■ *Grover E. Murray*
■ Studies in the American Southwest

D1714948

ALSO IN THE GROVER E. MURRAY STUDIES IN THE
AMERICAN SOUTHWEST SERIES

Cacti of the Trans-Pecos and Adjacent Areas
A. Michael Powell and James F. Weedin

Deep Time and the Texas High Plains: History and Geology
Paul H. Carlson

JAVELINAS

JAVELINAS

Jane Manaster

TEXAS TECH UNIVERSITY PRESS

This book is typeset in Galliard. The paper used in this book meets the minimum requirements of ANSI/NISO Z39.48-1992 (R1997). ∞

Designed by Lindsay Starr

Library of Congress Cataloging-in-Publication Data
Manaster, Jane.
Javelinas / by Jane Manaster.
    p. cm.—(Grover E. Murray studies in the American Southwest)
Summary: "Javelinas, or collared peccaries, are one of the most common wild animals of the American Southwest. Living in inhospitable areas, these little relatives of pigs and hippopotami have a public image long confused by folktales and misinformation. This book chronicles the javelinas' lifestyle and facts about their interactions with humans"—Provided by publisher.
    Includes bibliographical references.
    ISBN-13: 978-0-89672-577-5 (pbk. : alk. paper)
    ISBN-10: 0-89672-577-4 (pbk. : alk. paper) 1. Collared peccary. I. Title. II. Series.
    QL737.U59M36 2006
    599.63'4—dc22
                                                                    2005029155
Printed in the United States of America

06 07 08 09 10 11 12 13 14/ 9 8 7 6 5 4 3 2 1
TS

Texas Tech University Press
Box 41037
Lubbock, Texas 79409-1037 USA
800.832.4042
ttup@ttu.edu
www.ttup.ttu.edu

For Bailey and Hannah,

Kahlil and Avery,

and their cousins

yet to come

■

A Collared Peccary by any other name

would still be a javelina,

would deserve no respect—

some say, because

it has borrowed

the shape of pig

hide of wolf

hackles of porcupine

smell of skunk

bark of dog

rattle of snake.

So what's a poor javelina to do

to gain points in personal charm?

These are its favored things:

one elegant necklace of white,

two babies cherubic,

three curious toes on the hind feet,

and numberless prickly pear salads.

■

by JAN EPTON SEALE

from *Valley Ark: Life Along the Rio*

(McAllen, Texas: Knowing Press, 2005)

■ CONTENTS

• ACKNOWLEDGMENTS

Javelinas keep a low profile, and the few people I found who were familiar with their lifestyle generously shared their knowledge. Among them, the late Professor Lyle K. Sowls, who wrote the definitive scientific book, sent me special information; David Synatzske of the Chaparral Wildlife Management Area in South Texas has editing skills that match his abundant firsthand knowledge; Pat Durham with the Native American Fish and Wildlife Society explained the American Indian respect for animals; Lisa Engling and Jerry L. Cooke at Texas Parks and Wildlife helped figure out why javelinas roamed so far north of their native stomping ground; John Anderson rooted out historic photographs at the Texas State Library. Marilyn Caldwell suggested writing the book when she managed the Javelinas and Hollyhocks bookstore in Fort Davis. Special thanks (but with reservations) to Joe Bartosh, who lent me a mounted javelina head that growled silently but ferociously in my office until the work was done.

JAVELINAS

Introduction

AT NIGHTFALL the guests reach for their flashlights and creep from the Big Bend Lodge, closing the doors quietly behind them. They take to the paths before the moon rises, joining the footsteps of others on the same mission. This search is a first-time experience for most of the guests, and a muffled sneeze provokes a mildly irate "Bless you!" in the silent darkness, barely illuminated by the Pole Star and a scattering of other pinpricks in the vast sky above. Suddenly they become aware of less human sounds, snuffling, almost snorting beside the paths, and the guests whisper to each other, "It's *them*!"

A small herd of collared peccaries, or javelinas as they are known in these parts, is on the nightly prowl. Standing some twenty inches high, they pay no heed to the spectators as they move closer to the lodge in search of food scraps from the restaurant. On the way, their snouts probe carelessly for an easy snack to tide them over till they reach the real delicacies cast out from the kitchen. Eternal optimists, they never learn that the treats will be tied securely in garbage bags.

The animals are unaware of political boundaries imposed by humans. They roam across the Mexican border into the area of the Big Bend and the Trans-Pecos, the far western reaches of Texas, where the Rio Grande River dips southward, cupping the Big Bend National Park in the vast desert landscape lying beyond the Pecos River. Here wildlife abounds, though many creatures are too well camouflaged by the natural surroundings to be seen easily.

JAVELINAS

How can we explain the javelina's appeal? It is hardly beautiful, nor is it useful in contemporary human terms. Even when a foundling is adopted by humans, the neighbors are more likely to lock up their own pets than to put out the welcome mat. Like the biblical lilies of the field, they "toil not, neither do they spin"; yet they are an intrinsic part of America's Southwest regional landscape no less than the roadrunner, armadillo, or horned lizard, and as such they have won a place of affection.

Those who stop at the Big Bend, or in the Davis and Guadalupe mountains to the north, hope to take home tales of the wildlife. Each park entrance carries warnings of the occasional black bear and mountain lion that might be overly curious about the presence of a car or the tent pitched in its territory. Javelinas are reckoned a threat only to dogs, not to human visitors.

Collared peccaries, scientifically *Pecari tajacu*—or *Tayassu tajacu,* as they were listed until 1994—are known familiarly as javelinas in Texas, New Mexico, and Arizona. Because of the mystified looks this name often receives when used, it is probably uncommon, if not unknown, outside the animals' native range. It is pronounced *havaleena.* Perhaps it comes from the Spanish *jabalina,* meaning "spear," or the Arabic *jabaliy,* short for *khinzir jabaliy,* a mountain pig, a word most likely brought to the New World after the Moors introduced it to Spain. Further south, in Latin America, indigenous tribes have chosen dozens of other names for the three species of peccaries, all of which originated in the New World. Even in the United States the javelina is known by several names, with varying degrees of accuracy: the musk hog, wild hog, and desert hog to name but a few. Members of the greater community, when they refer to the animals at all, most often choose javelina and generally assume the animal is some kind of pig. In fact, the two branches—pigs and peccaries—although stemming from an early root, may have started out on their different paths as long as forty million years ago.

Javelinas exist in separated pockets across the southwestern United States in Texas, New Mexico, and Arizona. They stop short of California but can be found in Mexico, parts of Central America, and southward through Argentina. Below the United States border, starting at the southern Mexico isthmus, the javelina shares space with the larger white-lipped peccary (*Tayassu pecari*), whose range extends to a latitude midway through Uruguay. In 1972 the third species, the Chacoan peccary (*Catagonus wagneri*), largest in size and long thought to be extinct, was rediscovered in the Chaco, the isolated region where Bolivia, Paraguay, and Argentina come together.

The collared peccary is identified easily by a ring of lighter hair encircling its neck between an oversized head and sleek body. A single glance shows how dissimilar it is to members of the Suidae family such as the European boar, the African warthog, or the plain European "porker." Seen beside each other, familial physical differences become apparent. Peccaries have fewer toes. Their upper and lower canines are straight and vertical, unlike the curving ones of pigs and boars. The peccary makes do with a diminutive tail rather than the long, curling kind tacked onto the rear end of pigs. Other features also distinguish one family from the other, but none more than the peccary's dorsal scent gland. Many scientists have speculated on its purpose and eventually have agreed it may serve several functions, most of them social. No less an eminence than John J. Audubon wrote, "This part of the animal has been vulgarly supposed to be its navel," and scornfully rejected the idea.

Although their fossil remains are scattered throughout several states, the immediate history of javelinas in the Southwest is quite short. Scientists T. Knipe and G. I. Day suggest that javelinas were probably unknown in Arizona before the seventeenth century. Their image decorates none of the American Indian pottery there, nor is it recognized in regional folklore. In New Mexico they once roamed near the border with Texas, but apart from a few dozen seen occasionally in the southeastern section, they are now found mostly in the southwestern quadrant of the state. The animals have had a checkered past in Texas, and although at one time they roamed the northern and eastern part of the state, they now inhabit only the southern, south central, and southwestern counties. Their range in Arizona is expanding, and in recent years javelinas have been spotted as far north as the Mogollon Rim, several miles beyond the limit recorded by nineteenth-century observers.

Javelinas are quite predictable in their habitat selection and in the patterns of their diet and lifestyle. They live in herds that may number from a few individual animals to forty or fifty; food availability and "social space" requirements determine the size of the herd. Together they forage, rest, and socialize, often splitting into smaller groups to find more food, then regrouping later. Naturalists affirm that the animals are basically shy, though some nonscientists hold a different opinion. Charles E. Bendire, a U.S. army major who spent his off-duty hours hunting in the Chiricahua and Whetstone mountains and near the old San Xavier Mission in the Santa Cruz Mountains in the 1850s, recorded what he saw as an amusing incident, a servant held captive in a tree by a band of infuriated peccaries. Versions of this tale, with varying amounts of gory detail, spring up quite frequently throughout javelina territory. Less gullible park rangers suggest that a herd of javelinas, if disturbed, will scatter and run in every direction and whoever happens to be standing nearby is likely to be in the path of escape. On occasion, their poor eyesight and stubborn nature tend to predicate their behavior.

The present-day consensus is that javelinas favor a live-and-let-live approach. Especially in state and national parks, javelinas are too interested in what campers discard to worry about pursuing or attacking them. Dogs are at risk, perhaps because of their resemblance to predatory coyotes, and warnings are posted in all parks to keep dogs on a leash and away from the javelinas' shortsighted eyes.

As cities and suburbs grow and encroach on wildlife habitats and as environmental sensitivity increases, wild animals once prone to avoiding humans are losing their fear of human presence. In much of their former habitat, javelinas have joined deer in invading suburban yards and, like squirrels, raccoons, opossums, and rodents, fearlessly make their nocturnal or diurnal rounds. While they still remain wary of people in most areas, javelinas in some parts of Arizona have obliged city councils to warn residents not to encourage the animals' presence or familiarize them with the easy life enjoyed by domestic animals.

■ When alarmed, javelinas can move with surprising speed.
Wyman Meinzer.

ONCE, JAVELINAS seemed almost mythical. The desert Southwest was unknown territory to most people, and information about the animals that roamed there was sketchy, even apocryphal. In Texas javelinas were once sighted in places from which they have long since disappeared or where numbers have dwindled, especially in the eastern part of the state. Juan Brebel mentioned them in the list of animals he noted along the upper Red River in 1765; and Thomas Nuttall, whose travels are included in Thwaites' *Early Western Travels,* claimed to have seen them on the north side of the Red River north of Paris, Texas. Early Texas settler William DeWees was furious when "havalenas" killed his dogs near Hearne in Robertson County, Texas; and A. J. Pickett also saw them in Wharton County, east of their present range. Auguste Freteliere reported seeing them near Castroville, a community organized in the 1840s at the northern edge of today's range. Many more notations have been gathered and reported in historical compilations, some probably more hearsay than actual sightings.

In the nineteenth century, when explorers with one determination or another trekked toward the sunset, reports introduced unimagined flora and fauna to the English-speaking world. The kings of Spain had learned at least two centuries earlier about javelinas and other beasts of the field inhabiting the New World. In the United States travelers had no royal command to report their findings, but javelinas were described by army personnel on military or surveying forays, by boosters seeking company in the West, by travelers hoping for adventure or new trading markets, and by a handful of women who were setting up new homes or simply passing through.

Before television or photography became the means of capturing the exotic, globe-trotters took home fanciful descriptions of the animals they saw in their travels. Creatures now considered unremarkable seemed more menacing or endearing. Those who spotted groups of javelinas included descriptions in their catalogs of curiosities.

Often the letters and retrospective accounts tended to dramatize, but sometimes javelinas seemed downright puzzling. Should they be ignored or eaten? The early surveyors who enjoyed hunting in their spare time found javelina meat a generally satisfactory novelty, though none advocated it as a staple. Should javelinas be feared or befriended? The naturalist William P. Smith wrote about javelinas scaring settlers along the Brazos River before the 1833 floods. He trapped a pair of them in a hollow tree, secured the entrance, then cut into the tree trunk above them, dropped a noose round their necks, tied their legs and feet securely, and bound their jaws with cords. He considered them "the bravest animal of these forests, fearing neither man nor beast."

For some, the experience of being treed by a herd of furious animals with sharp tusks became a lifelong memory, and the number of the herd and the duration of the siege tended to increase with the telling. Others were skeptical. "Judging by the rapidity with which these little pigs can travel through the brush," commented Chapman Grant in his New York Zoological Bulletin article a few years into the twentieth century, "I believe it would be very difficult for an active man to climb a tree, even were there one at hand, before being overtaken. I have shot peccaries, and had a bunch of from 5 to 15 scurry past me under the brush in open formation. Those that passed near by would see me,

COYÁMETL O QUAUHCOYÁMETL

COYÁMETL O QUAUHCOYÁMETL

■ Drawings of collared peccaries from Francisco Hernandez, *Nova Plantarum, Animalium et Mineralium Mexicanorum* (Rome: 1651). *Courtesy Nettie Lee Benson Latin American Collection, University of Texas at Austin.*

and snap their tusks and raise their manes; and I believe that this helter-skelter hurry for safety is often mistaken for a charge, when really the little pigs are merely running in the direction in which they were headed when startled."

While some found javelinas wild and shy, trying their utmost to escape human intruders, others were convinced the "Mexican hog" was a most furious, untamable animal and was dangerous to encounter without sharp and sure weapons. Occasionally, a javelina seemed to have a dual personality. When Edgar Mearns cataloged the species of mammals along the north side of the Mexican border in the 1890s, he bought a tame animal from a Mexican lad, who had fondled and kissed it and who parted from it tearfully. "It followed us about in the camps, where, from its habit of rubbing against one, it received several hard kicks from frightened teamsters at night, which wrought such a change in its previously friendly disposition that no one could safely approach it." Finally, the animal was banished to the National Zoological Park, though whether with relief, regret, or a combination of both is not known.

Javelinas seem unperturbed by the presence of field biologists and researchers. When their surroundings are comfortable, they will resist the call of the wild. Audubon mentioned one living in a menagerie in Charleston in the 1840s that was "exceedingly gentle, taking its food from the hand, and allowing itself to be caressed even by strangers. It lies down in the manner of a pig, and next to giving it food, the greatest favour you can bestow on it is to scratch it with the hand or a stick." Audubon recalled how the javelina was "always most lively and playful on warm days. It appears to prefer Indian-corn, potatoes, bread and fruits, but like the domestic hog evinces no unwillingness to take any kind of food that is presented to it." The only two dislikes he noticed in the animal were cold weather and an intense aversion to dogs.

When James O. Pattie set out from Kentucky in the early 1830s to find success as a hunter and trapper, he more than compensated for his lack of education by his ability to embellish every escapade. He accompanied his father and a small party of similarly adventurous souls on a journey through central New Mexico. Fearsome skirmishes with American Indians alternated with periods of isolation and near-starvation, and the group was forced to shoot ravens and buzzards for food and even devoured a pet dog in order to survive. They killed many javelinas but, despite being famished, could never bring themselves to eat them. They were intimidated or repulsed by the species, "entirely different from our domestic swine. They are fox-colored, with a navel on their back, toward the back part of their bodies. . . . They yield an odor not less offensive than our polecat. . . . We measured one of their tusks, of a size so enormous, that I am afraid to commit my credibility, by giving the dimensions. They remain undisturbed by man and other animals, whether through fear or on account of their offensive odor, I am unable to say."

Charles C. Webber remembered a traumatic peccary hunt in 1854 in his series *Romance of Sporting* and supplied a picturesque image of the javelina: "This droll creature seems to be exactly the intermediate between the family of hedge-hogs and that of the wild boar, or common hog. Its general form, so far as the body is concerned, resembles rather more that of the hedge-hog, while its hair, which is about the average length of the bristles of the common hog, is thinly set in a rough skin, and flattened and sharp, as are the spines of the hedge-hog, and of the same bony consistence in appearance."

Captain Mayne Reid also delighted readers by spinning hunting tales and devoted a chapter to javelinas in his 1860 book *The Hunter's Feast,* appropriately subtitled *Conversations Around the Camp-fire.* He claimed, "I excel not in the chase, I excel not in a knowledge of natural history—but both I love." His enthusiasm was tempered by inaccuracy as he explained how javelinas were not killed for their flesh, skin, or sport but because they were tiresome, wreaking havoc in planted fields. Although he suggested they lived gregariously in herds through the winter, they chose to separate in "the season of love" and were seen only in pairs. He included a breathtaking account, credited to a Kentuckian at the campfire, about a herd of fierce javelinas who pounced in turn on the coiled body of a rattlesnake.

Later, but with the same wish to titillate the imagination, James H. Cook, who spent fifty years on the frontier as a cowboy, hunter, guide, scout, and ranchman, remembered large herds of javelinas in Texas. An old-timer told him a javelina in battle resembled, more than anything else, a "ball of hair with a butcher knife run through it."

In Texas between 1836 and 1845 boosters worked hard to bring money and additional immigrants to the new republic. William Bollaert, an inveterate traveler born in England in 1807, read William Kennedy's *Rise and Prospects for the Republic of Texas.* It gave him "a strange inkling to know this republic," and he rose to the challenge. He recorded his impressions in six diaries and two volumes of journals written between 1841 and 1844. His essay on game species contradicted Pattie's opinion of javelinas. They were, Bollaert wrote, "found generally in the low hollows of trees and shot; the meat is very good."

Bollaert's contemporary, Viktor Bracht, a German who spoke several languages, was chosen by his government to look after German interests in the New Braunfels colony in Central Texas. He became an American citizen and settled in Texas in 1848. After he explored the state, he wrote a detailed natural history to encourage settlers to take advantage of the economic potential afforded by the climate and geography. He saw plenty of javelinas:

> The entire hilly region of the West is infested by large herds
> of Mexican hogs, also called peccary or musk hogs. But
> these animals hide themselves so well in the thicket of the

river bottoms and in caves on the mountains that one gets to see them very seldom, although their fresh tracks may be seen at almost any time. Usually they flee when a person comes near them suddenly; but sometimes they attack the intruder of their wilderness, and are then unusually dangerous for dogs. When wounded, they become furious. Those that I have killed weighed between sixty and eighty pounds and made a fine roast. When the musk gland is not removed properly, the meat acquires an odious scent and taste.

An anonymous booster who published *A History of Texas, or, the Emigrant's Guide to the New Republic* in 1844 refuted an article in the *Encyclopedia Americana* that sug-

■ Hunting Peccaries in Texas—A Bear Hunt Without the Metaphysics, from C. W. Webber, *The Hunter-Naturalist: Romance of Sporting, or Wild Scenes and Wild Hunters* (Philadelphia: J. B. Lippincott, 1867). Courtesy Texas State Library and Archives Commission.

gested the peccary range was limited to South America. They could be found, he wrote, in the bottoms of all Texas rivers where the timber is large and the place densely wooded; but they were rarely domesticated in spite of occasionally being reared as pets. He believed the reason was not simply their offensive smell, but also their "destructive propensities," which led them to destroy whole litters of domestic pigs and, "when old and strong enough, even large hogs." He did not like the way they expressed their feelings with "the same disagreeable grunt" as the hog, but he admired their resourcefulness. "When a hunter approaches their burrow, one of the inmates is found standing at the entrance guarding it from aggression. From this position he cannot be driven by fright or even wounds. When he is shot down another immediately supplies his place, and with equal courage maintains his post. When he falls another comes, and so they continue to do till all except the very young ones are killed."

Several educated women ventured westward and were attracted to frontier life. They found it a welcome alternative to the restrictions imposed by their middle-class existence. Mary Austin Holley was raised in New England and married a clergyman who later became president of Transylvania University in Lexington, Kentucky. When he died, she contacted her younger cousin in Texas. He was the *empresario* Stephen F. Austin, then struggling to attract Anglo-American settlers to his large land grant. He had been fond of Mary since childhood and now offered her a league of land for herself. The 4,428 acres near his own plantation could be hers, he promised, if she came to Texas to claim it. In 1831 she set out for the frontier with her emotionally disturbed son and wrote about the territory soon to achieve its independence from Mexico. In her chapter on natural history, she spared a few lines for the javelina: "The Peccary or Mexican hog is even yet occasionally met with, on the frontiers, in considerable gangs. They will boldly attack a man, and are considered more dangerous than any other wild animal in Texas. The pecari [*sic*] is of a greyish color, and the ordinary size of the domestic hog; its bristles stand erect. It is armed with tusks, several inches in length, which curl back from the under jaw, and its aspect is altogether very ferocious."

About the same time, Ann Raney Coleman came with her family to Texas from England and enjoyed helping the "Texians" on their quest for independence. In her old age she sifted through her diaries and compiled a history of her long life for her niece. A spirited picture of life on the frontier, it was published almost a century later in 1971. She recalled an event when accompanied by her companion "Mr. A."—who makes but a single appearance in the diary—when they encountered a group of so-called Mexican hogs.

> I noticed how small and short their legs were, when presently one or two bristled up at me, gnashed their tusks which were very long and large, and came after me, I took to my heels and ran as fast as I could. . . . At the creek I was met by Mr. A. in his shirt and drawers, with a sack of corn on his back, one or two other men in like condition, some having their shirt off and their drawers which they were trying to put on when I got to the creek, our screams having attracted their attention. . . . I told Mr. A. that we had been followed by Mexican hogs and that his wife was on the road running for her life, and to make haste as she was nearly exhausted. It is hard to determine whether I was more alarmed at the Mexican hogs or the men in a state of nudity for they cut a singular figure.

She recovered fast, but next day the doctor said her plump companion's heart was injured "by the fat melting over it."

The most reliable early accounts came from military personnel and the scientists who accompanied them. In 1854, engineers in Colonel S. W. Kearny's expedition set off from Kansas to survey the Gadsden Purchase boundary, mapping the region from the Rio Grande to the Pacific. The expedition's zoological data were collected and published in 1859 by Spencer F. Baird, who later became Secretary of the Smithsonian Institution. With regard to javelinas, he included remarks made on the earlier Whipple Expedition by Dr. C. B. R. Kennerley, who saw the animals at only one point west of the Rio Grande, at an abandoned Mexican ranch just south of the Arizona border. The same year, a medical doctor spotted javelinas near Fort Buchanan on Sonoita Creek ten miles north of present-day Patagonia, Arizona.

In 1892 Edgar Alexander Mearns, a major and surgeon in the U.S. Army, was assigned by the War Department to act as medical officer for the International Boundary Survey. He wrote a descriptive catalog of the area's mammal species in his "Mammals of the Mexican Boundary of the United States," published in the *U.S. National Museum Bulletin No. 56* in 1907. Lt. Col. J. W. Barlow, the senior commissioner, authorized Mearns to carry out the biological survey as long as it did not add to the cost of the project nor take him from his official medical duties. At the end of his quest he dispatched thirty thousand specimens of flora, fauna, and fossils to the U.S. National Museum, and attributed his success to the lasting good health of the party.

Mearns saw numerous javelinas. As the party moved westward from the Rio Grande across New Mexico and then Arizona, he first saw the hides of javelinas killed in the Apache Mountains near Monument 40 on the Mexican boundary line. Later, he took specimens in the San Luis Mountains, where the javelinas' habitat reached from the lower timberline to the top summits, and in the abundant vegetation of the surrounding plains. They also ranged in the Guadalupe, Santa Cruz, Pajarito, and Huachuca mountains and the valley of the San Bernardino River. Hunting parties from Fort Bowie found their quarry in the oak scrub around Monument 64, which was marked by the timberline at the east base of the San Luis Mountains. "Major E. K. Otey," wrote Mearns, "found peccaries in the Mule Mountains of southern Arizona, and General Crook found them in the Tonto Basin where the writer saw their tracks as far north as Pine and Fossil Creeks in Central Arizona. On the Mexican Boundary Line the species was found by us as far west as the Sonoya Valley, near the Mexican town of Santo Domingo, beyond which point and the Pacific Ocean no trace of it was seen, although it reaches the Gulf of California further south in the strip of country named Seriland by Dr. W. J. McGee."

Soldiers stationed in forts across the frontier counted hunting among their few recreational activities. With the end of American Indian depredations and the arrival of railroads, the forts became obsolete, but hunters continued to tread the desert paths.

Legend was still being mingled with fact when an 1884 article in *Farm and Ranch* magazine gave a vivid account of two colleagues who climbed a tree on the Wichita River with their Winchesters to stay clear of a herd of javelinas. With the animals some thirty yards distant, the two men fired simultaneously, and the javelinas charged.

> When they arrived at the tree they bit it each in turn, and then glancing up, squatted and fixed upon us a dozen pair of eyes small as peas and blazing with fierce purpose and fury intense. One by one we shot them, and they fell, one by one, and died each willing and ready to go. . . . Presently only one was left alive amid a dozen corpses, and there he sat, brown, bristling, furious, foaming with raging

life, courting death, unmindful of the blood that damp-
ened the grass about him, indifferent of the fate of com-
rades—a very epitome of hate.

Around the same time the *San Antonio Express* ran a
series of articles by a well-known local lawyer, Judge Moses,
in which he intrigued readers with his personal recollections
of encroaching urban sprawl. "When running mustangs we
would often get out of provision, and would have to pick
out some of our best men to rope wild cattle or *javalis* (as
the Mexican wild hogs are called). These latter were very
abundant in the country at that time, and are, in fact, plentiful yet. Though hard to lasso until one gets the knack of it,
they are easy enough to rope when the manner of doing so
is learned: and though it is true of *javalis* that when one is
wounded and squeals, the drove will stay around and fight
fiercely, yet we have never regarded them as a very dangerous animal. I have seen Mexicans often ride into a herd of
them and kill two or three with their machetes and even with
the butt of a loaded quirt. In fact, I have done as much
myself. The meat of the javelinas, though not to say very
excellent, is not unsavory, and that of a young sow, seasoned
with the sauce of hunger, goes mighty well."

Javelinas have edged their way into the folklore of the
Southwest. They have also continued to be targeted for
sport and survival among a growing number of hunters in
the region. South of the Rio Grande border, and far more in
South America, collared peccaries continue to be hunted for
their hides and for food, and their numbers appear to be
dwindling there. North Americans tend to reject the lean,
tough meat, which bears little resemblance to pork. Impacts
of the hide trade, which reached a peak north of the Rio
Grande in the first years of the twentieth century, led early
environmentalists to call a halt to the slaughter and seek protection for the animal.

JAVELINAS

Hunting native and exotic game continues to be a popular recreation; and while javelinas head few popularity lists, the numbers taken each year are not to be ignored, as they, too, contribute to the substantial management funds engendered by the sport. Indeed, in Arizona they are the third most popular big game species, and hunters must draw for a permit to hunt them. Money from federal excise taxes on firearms, ammunition, hunting permits, and license fees support wildlife conservation programs. Hunting generates income for those who provide hunting opportunities, especially in Texas where 97 percent of the land is privately owned. This income enables millions of acres to be maintained as wildlife habitat—land that might otherwise be committed to less wildlife-friendly uses.

Gone are the market hunting days when dogs were used to corner the javelinas and hunters clubbed them to death. Even in an exchange of hunting yarns, Jack O'Connor's enjoyable memories recorded in *Game in the Desert* would today draw gasps of shock. Few would write now, as he did in the 1930s, "I must admit that banging my javelina on the head did give me something of a thrill. It was hunting such as our caveman ancestors once did, and it was not without danger." Present-day hunting laws and hunter ethics demonstrate a higher regard and respect for wildlife.

Range ∎

WHEN THE WEST was being settled, species of wildlife that posed a threat or danger to human settlement were quickly distinguished from the harmless. Ranchers and hunters who profited from the sale of javelina hides significantly reduced the animals' range. Sheep ranchers also killed javelinas, believing they targeted their flocks. More recently, migration to the Sunbelt led to developing new highways and infrastructure, again changing the landscape. Human population shift, together with the transformation of agricultural practices over the past two generations, leaves native animals living in a contracted range. Despite these dangers to wildlife, resource management has contributed to an increase in the number of javelinas and in some instances their geographic range, although urbanization retains an increasing impact on them.

Texas

∎ Texas has by far the largest population of javelinas in the United States. The latest figures indicate about two hundred thousand living in the state, spread over a region covering eighty-eight thousand square miles. They range south from the Balcones Escarpment down into the Rio Grande Plain and across to the West Texas Rolling Plains and the Trans-Pecos mountains and basins.

Historically javelinas ranged throughout South Texas, northward through the Pecos Valley to the New Mexico

Sand Hills, across the plains toward San Angelo (a leading wool and mohair market), and then southeastward toward Kerrville in the Hill Country. Travelers on the Texas Pacific Railroad saw plenty of them beside the track near Odessa, the shipping and refining center of the Permian Basin oil field. They were sighted in the sand belt to the north of Monahans, a small town that served as a supply center for ranchers until the Winkler oil field brought prosperity. There, javelinas feasted on the acorns that dropped from the abundant oaks.

By the close of the twentieth century the northern boundary of their distribution extended from Port Lavaca in the southeast, up through the brush country toward San Antonio and Ozona, then west to Fort Stockton, and back southward to the border town of Presidio. Although the area is sparsely populated, new industrial plants, the maquiladoras, provide jobs on the Mexican side of the Rio Grande; and as development encroaches on the region, the javelinas may find their options restricted. They have been edged out of the eastern reaches of the state already, where they once haunted the palmetto and cane growths beside the San Bernard River in Brazoria County and crowded along the Brazos River in McLennan County, near Waco.

A map of current javelina distribution in Texas shows the northern range of the most abundant population curving northwestward from the Gulf of Mexico, presenting a stretch of counties where the animal may be hunted year-round. To the north, following the same contour, the neighboring counties allow seasonal harvesting. Further north, an apparent anomaly identifies five counties where hunting is permitted for a limited season. They are separated from the principal range by a boundary spanning two counties. This discrete range is the result of restocking by the Texas Parks and Wildlife Department, which brought three dozen animals to Wilbarger County in the 1957–1958 season and subsequently thirty more to Archer County. The peccaries found the area compatible, and the rate of reproduction was sufficient to permit hunting in these and adjacent counties. At least one animal was harvested early in the year 2000—doubtless to the hunter's surprise—over the state border in Oklahoma.

New Mexico

■ In New Mexico the occurrence of javelinas has undergone change. The animals were once a familiar sight in the southeastern part of the state, but this population dwindled as ranchers began to buy acreage to the north of Monahans, Texas. In 1912 environmentalist Aldo Leopold, then a forest ranger, reported a herd of about twenty-five javelinas near present-day Big Hatchet Peak. They were also spotted from time to time in the Peloncilla Mountains and Cloverdale Hills.

Javelinas have since begun to move eastward through Hidalgo County to the Tres Hermanas in Luna County and up into the San Francisco River and Gila River drainage basins. In 1954 wildlife managers suspected the population might be growing when a single javelina was sighted just west of Carlsbad Caverns National Park. Before many years had passed, javelinas populated an area of no less than eighteen thousand square miles. Mostly, they range in Hidalgo, Grant, Catron, Otero, and Eddy counties of New Mexico.

Some reports claim javelinas have disappeared from the southeastern corner of the state, but several dozen, perhaps even a few hundred, still roam the Roswell area, though the population is insufficient to allow hunting. If the habitat continues to be hospitable, those herds will probably increase naturally.

Arizona

■ In Arizona javelinas range over about a third of the state. Their distribution is extending northward, radiating from the southeast quadrant close to the New Mexico boundary. No visual representations of them have occurred in any of the American Indian archaeological sites in the region, which strongly suggests their arrival is fairly recent. Neither physical remains nor artistic images can be found in the Tonto National Monument ruins, which commemorate a fourteenth-century civilization. They are equally absent from Snaketown, a site near Florence on the Gila River that dates back even further and sustained an American Indian community until the middle of the fifteenth century. Today, the animals are quite common in both areas. Communities of Sobaipuri Indians lived along the Upper San Pedro Mountains between 1400 and 1700, but they left no trace of evidence that they knew javelinas.

In addition to ranging over these three southwestern states, the javelinas live in the adjacent states across the Mexican border. Ignaz Pfefferkorn and Juan Nentvig, eighteenth-century Jesuit missionaries who worked in the state of Sonora across the United States border in Mexico, noted that the Sonoran Indians ate musk hogs. This information strongly suggests javelinas began to make their way north from Mexico into Arizona during the late eighteenth or early nineteenth century. In a later report, published a generation or two after Pfefferkorn and Nentvig, javelinas are not even mentioned, although other game is described. Presumably the explorers did not hunt them for food.

Today javelinas are increasing their range to within a fifty-mile radius of Nogales on the Mexican border. They are found in the Bradshaw and Ajo mountains and in the Verde Valley and upper Agua Fria drainage. They have also moved in a northwesterly direction to the Hieroglyphic, Harqua-

■ Javelinas lounging in the shade. Scratchboard by Larry Toschik, from Knipe, *The Javelina in Arizona*.

hala, and Weaver mountains, where they were unknown before the 1950s. During the 1950s resource managers began transplanting animals from the southern edge of their range up into the Tucson Mountains immediately west of the city. For years the animals' northern limit was the southern edge of the Mogollon Rim, an escarpment crossing the state. Now they have reached the rim, and their statewide distribution occupies well over forty thousand square miles.

The three states inhabited by javelinas share an arid environment. Despite this generalization, habitats differ dramatically within and among southern Texas, western Texas, New Mexico, and Arizona. The climate, altitude, and vegetation vary considerably from one area to the next. Beyond the border, in Central and South America, the differences are even greater, and collared peccaries roam through humid forests. Such extremes affirm their adaptability.

Javelina Kin

■ Javelinas share the name "peccary" with two other species in the New World. The white-lipped peccary, *Tayassu pecari,* lives alongside the collared peccary in the Amazon basin. Larger than the javelina, *T. pecari* ranges from Veracruz and Oaxaca in southern Mexico to Entre Rios in northern Argentina and Rio Grande do Sul in Brazil. It generally inhabits lowland forests at sea level but is also found in the lower montane forests covering the eastern slope of the Andes to an altitude of about sixty-three hundred feet and in mountainous reaches in Venezuela and Guatemala. Its preferred habitat is tropical rain forest, but it seems comfortably at home in more arid areas such as the Gran Chaco of Paraguay and the Venezuelan savanna.

The white-lipped peccary, so called because the chin, cheeks, and sides of its muzzle are white or cream-colored, grows to an average of sixty-two pounds. It is the only land mammal in the neotropics to roam in large herds, living in groups of a hundred or more. Its five subspecies are spread out across nineteen Latin American countries, and its home range can be as large as eighty square miles. Peccaries are omnivorous and will feed on fruits, invertebrates, small vertebrates, fungi, and carrion. Researchers believe that as the peccaries eat and disperse seeds in their wanderings, they play a significant role in the ecology of tropical forests.

The threats to *T. pecari* are the fragmentation and destruction of their habitat brought about by agriculture and cattle ranching and by deforestation programs. In Central America, years of civil war have wrought a two-pronged hazard. Not only has the heavily damaged terrain encroached on animal habitats, but more dramatically the armies dependent on wild game for their subsistence have slaughtered large numbers with automatic weapons.

In 1972 a remarkable creature was reported in the

remote Gran Chaco region of Paraguay, northern Argentina, and eastern Bolivia. A team of scientific researchers headed by Ralph M. Wetzels of the University of Connecticut was bewildered to find that the animal, locally known as a *tagua,* was in fact a species of peccary believed to be extinct. Also known as the Chacoan peccary, *Catagonus wagneri* is larger than both other species. The small herds rove across the flat plain amid thorn forest, swaths of savanna, parkland, marsh, and gallery forest. Their dietary mainstay is cactus, but they forage for other vegetation. They supplement their forage intake with naturally occurring salt licks and the mineral-rich soil. Tragically, the existence of these peaceable animals is endangered. They are on the 1996 Red List of Threatened Animals published by the IUCN (International Union for the Conservation of Nature and Natural Resources) and listed as an Appendix 1 species by CITES (the Convention of International Trade in Endangered Species of Wild Fauna and Flora). In the face of increased demand for agriculture and cattle pasture, much of the uncultivated Chaco habitat will be destroyed.

Habitat and Diet

WHEN VIEWED from the air, the rural stretches of the southwestern states appear to be barren desert. At ground level, the reality seems not altogether different, for without the economic overlay of cattle ranching and a few areas of managed parkland, the region is harsh. As elsewhere, latitude and climate combine to dictate the landscape and the vegetation; only amid the hills and mountains is the air fresher and less enervating. Javelinas share this challenging environment with mule deer, white-tailed deer, and other resilient wildlife.

In the heat of the day, even the keenest naturalist might have difficulty spotting javelinas in this wide-open terrain. They hide in cat-claw thickets, cling to the shadowy hollows of deep, rocky canyons, or camouflage themselves in the inhospitable thorny cactus and chaparral. Folklorist and naturalist J. Frank Dobie, one of Texas's favorite sons, wrote little about javelinas beyond noting that, along with Mexican or blue quail (*Callipepla squamata*) and the various rattlesnakes (*Crotalus* spp.), they were the most numerous form of wildlife in the thickets of *brasada,* or brush, growing between the Nueces river and the Rio Grande.

In order to survive, javelinas need not only food but also adequate cover for protection and comfort. Vegetative cover is vital as protection from predators. In some places javelinas rely on the dense and interwoven growth of the chaparral. In others they will hide themselves amid acres of coarse sacaton grass when they rest in the heat of the day. The cover is also important to provide shade and relief from the high temperatures common to desert regions.

Commonly the Suidae (Old World pigs) and the Tayassuidae peccaries of Central America live in forested or swampy surroundings. In the equatorial rain forests of South America, peccaries find space to rest in deep burrows, often under tree roots. In the Southwest, javelinas thrive in a surprisingly varied environment, even taking advantage of caves and shaded hollows on the arid terrain when plant life is particularly sparse. The key to their adaptation is being able to use every feature of their immediate surroundings.

This adaptability is clear in Big Bend National Park, which is located in the Chihuahuan Desert and offers acceptable habitat to javelinas. The Chisos Mountains tower above an area of low desert and profuse riparian vegetation sustained by the Rio Grande. Javelinas are just one of almost eighty mammal species roaming this diverse vegetative community, which also includes seventy varieties of cactus. The park lies to the west of the Pecos River, and rainfall in the mountains and basins of the eighteen-million-acre region averages a mere eight inches a year. Only the most drought-resistant vegetation is tough enough to survive, with lechuguilla, ocotillo, yucca, cenizo, and other arid-land plants amid the prevailing yeso, chino, and tobo grass. The species of trees vary from one elevation to the next, with junipers, small oaks, and pinyon pine giving way to ponderosa pine, Douglas fir, Arizona cypress, quaking aspen, and big tooth maple. Elevations above eight thousand feet are hospitable to fewer and fewer trees.

The Rio Grande Plain lies south of the city of San Antonio and down to the river that defines the border with Mexico. Although covered partly by prairie, much of the land, called the South Texas Brush Country, is javelina friendly, with a crowded cover of small trees and shrubs such as mesquite, dwarf oak, catclaw, guajillo, huisache, blackbrush, and cenizo. Prickly pear and other cactuses are plentiful. Brush Country is often referred to as chaparral or the *monte,* the regional Spanish term for dense brush. Further west, the twenty-one million acres comprising the South Texas Plains also have a dense covering of brush, with thickets crowding along the ridges and streams. According to Jerry Cooke, a former field biologist with the Texas Parks and Wildlife Department, javelinas and deer have moved in where cattle have overgrazed the grassland and the changed habitat has become dominated by brush, cactuses, and forbs.

In Arizona yellow pine forests and woodlands flourish at five thousand feet on the mountains of the Sonora Desert, while at lower elevations the density of the chaparral almost rebuffs sunlight, and vegetation in the canyons and *bajadas* affords camouflage for javelinas. Mesquite, coma, brazil, blackbrush, black persimmon, white brush, granjeno (the spiky hackberry), guajillo, and live oak shinnery cover great patches of land. Elsewhere, cactuses and succulents cling to the sandy soil and edge the outcroppings of rock.

G. I. Day, researching javelinas in Arizona, identified eight habitats of varying degrees of use by javelinas. Over a third of the javelinas in the state live in the Sonora Desert scrub. The southwestern segment, along the Colorado River washes, has creosote bush, bursage, saltbrush, desert thorn, and mesquite growing at altitudes ranging from one hundred to three thousand feet. A wide variety of desert plants grow at elevations from five hundred to four thousand feet. These altitudes are the home of the saguaro cactus. A second and far smaller area of desert scrub lies in the Chihuahuan Desert to the southeast. Another one-third of the state's population of javelinas is found at altitudes between thirty-five hundred and five thousand feet in the desert grassland, which is partially invaded by shrubs and cactuses.

Contrasting with the desert habitats of Arizona, two areas of conifer forest, predominantly juniper and ponderosa

■ Javelinas on the trail. Scratchboard by Larry Toschik, from Knipe,
The Javelina in Arizona.

pines, grow in the San Carlos Apache Indian Reservation and
just short of the Mogollon Rim to an altitude of seventy-five
hundred feet. Here, though, the weather is changeable and
food in short supply, making it a marginal choice for the peccaries. In the south the montane conifer forest rises to a similar altitude, and the temperatures are too cold in winter for
survival of javelinas.

Javelinas are also found in the southern evergreen woodlands, which are crowded with dense stands of oak, pine, and
juniper. In some cases, heavy cover is not beneficial and can
offer too much of a good thing at serious cost. As the evergreen shrubs can be virtually impenetrable, they provide
excellent cover but insufficient food. The smaller area of
riparian deciduous forest offers ideal habitat with adequate
food, water, and cover, but exists only along streams and at

the foot of the canyons crisscrossing the paths from the montane forests to the desert floor.

In New Mexico, where javelina distribution is more limited, pinyon, mountain mahogany, buckbrush, skunkbrush, and ponderosa pine grow among the junipers and oak from five thousand to sixty-four hundred feet. Mesquite flourishes between whitethorn, catclaw, prickly pear, ocotillo, and mescal at elevations ranging from forty-three hundred to sixty-two hundred feet.

According to T. Knipe, javelinas on most Texas and Arizona ranges favor prickly pear (*Opuntia* spp.). For part of the year the cactus supplies more than half their diet and most of the water they need. In some spots javelinas are blamed for the spread of prickly pear, while elsewhere their gnawing is thought to prevent the spread. Javelinas deserve little of the blame thrown at them for trampling and destroying crops as the guilty parties are the larger feral hogs that often share their habitat. Some ranchers intersperse brush with strips of prickly pear, so food and shelter for javelinas are both close at hand.

Day writes that javelinas on prickly pear diets would need to consume 20 percent of their body weight daily in order to meet sufficient protein needs. During dry seasons cactus is often the only food available, and the heavy consumption necessitated by the absence of alternatives frequently causes diarrhea. Lyle K. Sowls points out that javelinas may risk renal failure from the build-up of oxalic acid that may result when they are forced to overeat the cactus. Captive javelinas run into an additional health problem on inadequate diets, as they become immunodeficient when malnourished. Inadequate nourishment may contribute to bronchial congestion and likely other sicknesses both in captivity and in the wild. Javelinas intuitively supplement the prickly pear when possible with mast, notably acorns and other nuts and forbs, and they often root

■ During dry seasons cactus—thorns and all—is often the only food available. *Wyman Meinzer.*

out tubers and rhizomes from several inches below ground. In winter mesquite and ebony beans complement the prickly pear, and in Arizona javelinas will compete with deer for saguaro cactus. Javelinas also enjoy salt licks, and they will chew on old bones or antlers and pieces of desert tortoise shells, intuitively supplementing their diet to provide calcium and trace minerals.

■ Young boy feeding a javelina. *Courtesy Texas State Library and Archives Commission.*

In southern Texas javelinas feed on prickly pear, mast from mesquite and other brush, and forbs when available. Succulents such as lechuguilla and century plants often replace prickly pear in the western, more arid portions of Texas, where they may be consumed more for their water content than their nutritional value. As rainfall in the desert Southwest generally averages only ten to fourteen inches a year, vegetation responds quickly to sudden and unexpected desert precipitation. Javelinas, able to get by for a while on plants that absorb and retain water from the heaviest rainfalls, find themselves surrounded by new riches.

Although omnivorous, javelinas prefer forbs, fruits, and beans such as those of huisache and mesquite. In comparison with their cousins in the tropics, javelinas in desert environs fare poorly in their food options. In the rain forest they broaden their dietary base with animal protein and whatever their browsing snouts happen upon. In the southwestern United States, they are satisfied with less variety, eating various beans and mast to fulfill protein needs. In some places they root out dried mesquite beans from pack rat nests. Once they have made their way through the javelina's digestive tract, the seeds contained within these beans germinate and grow, contributing to the spread of that plant.

In *Javelina Research and Management in Arizona,* Day explains that unlike deer, javelinas cannot stand on their hind legs to feed; and despite being able to nibble away on large barrel cactus while standing upright, catching their balance with their forelegs, in captivity they are unable to reach bowls or other food containers set above their four-legged height. The verdict is still out on whether javelinas need water to supplement the supply found in cactuses and succulents. Day describes seeing them frequently slaking their thirst at the dozens of Arizona's "guzzlers," the roadside catchments filled by runoff and in dry spells sometimes filled by water trucks. They make their way to any potholes, springs, or even retention dams within reach. Although livestock drinking troughs are often inaccessible, the little animals seem to enjoy finding one that is overfilled or has sprung a leak.

As land use patterns have changed, peccaries have learned to seek out food grown as crops. Like deer, they are becoming an urban problem in some areas and singularly unwelcome visitors. Once they overcome a natural shyness and learn what treats are in store at public park garbage cans, they grow confident to the point of audacity. They have become shameless beggars at campgrounds and have no compunction about sharing other animals' salt and mineral licks.

Environmental hazards in their habitat contribute to mortality, which comes in different guises, from soaring rap-

JAVELINAS

tors to speeding automobiles. They wander onto train tracks and get caught in steel traps set for more destructive wildlife. In the past, range cowboys made sport of shooting them, even taking bets on how many they could fell with a single loading of their six-guns.

Javelinas suffer many diseases as well. In the wild their carcasses are often found too late for the cause of death to be determined, but respiratory infections are sometimes respon- sible in winter in the snowy northern reaches. Parasites fur- ther weaken animals vulnerable during periods of food shortage. From time to time epidemics occur. Two out- breaks of javelina encephalitis, a highly contagious disease akin to canine distemper, claimed hundreds of peccaries in Arizona and Texas in the late 1980s. Sowls has spelled out the risk of diarrhea and renal failure for wild animals, including javelinas, that rely on prickly pear for their main food. Among older peccaries, infections from worn-down teeth can lead to septicemia.

On the other hand, javelinas appear to resist several dis- eases, such as brucellosis, foot-and-mouth disease, rabies, and pseudorabies, that take a toll among domesticated ani- mals sharing their habitat. Young javelinas, though more sus- ceptible to bacterial intestinal infections than their elders, die more frequently from accidents or by falling victim to preda- tors than from disease. In the United States javelinas fall prey to mountain lions (cougars or pumas) and at the northern edge of their range to black bears. A herd of javelinas is strong enough to repulse coyotes and bobcats, and even individual animals can ward off most attacks. Golden eagles, like other predators, choose to focus their attacks on the youngest juveniles, which are helpless when targeted.

Despite surrounding hardships, the life span of a typical javelina in the wild is about ten years. They are physically equipped to cope with their marginal environment, surviving conditions few mammals must confront.

SUPERFICIALLY, no physical characteristics differ-
entiate the javelinas living in South and Central America
from those in the more arid and often mountainous terrain
of Texas, New Mexico, and Arizona. The animal adapts to a
variety of habitats and is equipped to survive from sea level
to an altitude of several thousand feet, with a digestive
system and teeth able to accommodate available local diet.
Adult males and females weigh on average between forty and
sixty pounds. The female is slightly smaller than the male,
but even near at hand the only apparent difference is in the
area of the sexual organs.

Javelinas in New Mexico are slightly larger and lighter in
coloration than those found in Texas, but as the two groups
tend not to mingle and the larger ones live in dense vegetation, not much opportunity exists for comparison in the
wild. A few possible subspecies of javelinas live in the United
States, such as *Pecari tajacu sonoriensis* in southern Arizona
and a small segment of southwestern New Mexico, and *P.
tajacu angulatus* in South Texas, although according to
Knipe their particular distinctions are still undecided.

Peccaries and distantly related pigs and hogs belong to
the order Artiodactyla, or even-hoofed mammals, and the
suborder Suiformes. Two families of the suborder are Suidae,
representing pigs or hogs, and Tayassuidae, the peccaries; the
third related family, perhaps surprisingly to nonscientists, is
Hippopotamidae, the hippopotamuses.

Both Suidae and Tayassuidae species have disklike snouts

and live in herds in the wild. They have a similar but not identical body shape. Among differences, peccaries invariably have thirty-eight teeth, while their relatives may have thirty-four or forty-four, according to species. Peccaries have two-inch straight tusks, their canines, well-developed for cutting and slashing, whereas pigs and hogs have longer, curving ones. Pigs have a long and curly tail, but peccary tails are almost an apology, what Seton termed "a mere knob." The peccary has six to nine tail vertebrae compared to the pig's twenty to twenty-three. In a comparative table of the species, Sowls identifies a complex stomach for the Tayassuidae and a simple one for the Suidae.

Peccaries have four toes on each front foot, only two of which touch the ground when they walk. The hind feet have only three toes with one dew claw on each foot. These small hooves are keratinous in front, like other hooves, horns, and nails, and have a soft and pliable pad in back. Although their feet allow the animals to cover half a mile in little over an hour, javelinas rarely run unless scared, in which case they can take off at a sprint. On occasion, they swim.

Javelina coloration varies according to age and season. Newborn piglets are striped and covered with a soft reddish-brown hair replaced by bristles after a few weeks. The collar is already visible at birth, and a dark strip extends from the back of the head down to the scent gland. During the winter, adults are dark brown, almost black, but peppered with white specks. Early in the spring they begin their annual molt, and as the bristles fall out over the following weeks, the javelinas sometimes begin to look like albinos. Even when the new bristles grow in, they are gray during the summer and do not darken until fall. Bristles are between five and six inches long, noticeably longer on the back than on the shoulders, chest, or stomach. Tough skin, together with these bristles, provides a good barrier to harmful scratches from the thorny vegetation that often grows where they live. Javelinas and white-lipped peccaries both look sleeker than the Chacoans as their bristles are shorter.

The scent gland distinguishing peccaries is readily visible as a raised area of skin on the back measuring about four to six inches in length and less than four inches in width. It has a nipple under half an inch across set in the center. The strong odor of the gland's excretion has been kindly, if inaccurately, described as like cheese or chicken soup. It seems to keep insects away and fits into a number of behavioral contexts.

In addition to visible characteristics, javelinas have clearly defined sensory strengths and weaknesses. For instance, they probably cannot see a moving object from further than a hundred yards away. When they appear to be watching an object, their keen hearing is more likely coming into play. Vision is even less effective in piglets; one study found that young javelinas captive for eight days and moved from an indoor to an outdoor pen were unable to find their way back without a light to guide them. Javelinas see poorly, smell and hear well, and have a catholic sense of taste that combines well with their skill at nosing out food supplies beneath the ground. Beyond the five senses, they communicate with an extensive repertoire of sounds allowing them to convey a remarkable range of messages. Their grunts, mutterings, popping of teeth, and barking define their behavior.

Peccaries have a certain appeal. Their appearance and behavior captivated Francisco Hernandez as he described them in his *Nova Plantarum, Animalium et Mineralium Mexicanorum*, his natural history of Mexico written for King Philip II of Spain and published in Rome in 1651:

> The *coyametl*, which some call the *quauhcoyametl* because it is wild, others *quauhtlacoyametl* and others *quauhpezotli*, looks similar to the wild boar in our country, but it is much smaller and notable for a navel (as the local people call it) which is on its back, and which has a watery

flow when the animal is taken by the feet; but it isn't a true navel. . . . It is ferocious and screams when captured, but once it is tamed it is peaceable and makes up to everyone in the house, earning their affection. The meat is similar to hog boar but tougher and less tasty; the flesh is tough, with dark and light meat mixed. It feeds on roots, acorns, and other wild fruits, and also worms, earthworms and similar insects found in humid regions, lakes, and swamps. It also destroys crops when one doesn't take care to scare them away. They move in herds. They are also tempted by all the food one gives to domestic animals. The claws on their font and back feet are different, some broader and the others shorter.

The javelina received an admiring testimonial from Homer Shantz back in 1930: "The African wort [sic] hog, bush pig and great black forest hog are homely creatures compared with the peccary. This animal . . . is an unusually attractive looking beast. The hair is coarse but clean and handsome with its crossbars of light color."

Not all descriptions have been so flattering. Trying to decide whether to take up her cousin's suggestion to settle in Texas, Mary Austin Holley wrote, with only limited accuracy, that the javelina was "the ordinary size of the domestic hog; its bristles stand erect. It is armed with tusks, several inches in length, which curl back from the under jaw, and its aspect altogether is very ferocious."

Behavior ∎

THE BIOLOGY of peccaries is straightforward compared with their behavior, which is sometimes open to interpretation. The view of wildlife resource managers, for example, will differ from that of nervous bystanders in wilderness areas.

If one recognizes—as the fictional Dr. Dolittle did—that animals have their own means of communication, then the various javelina grunts, clicks, and barks have an intelligible pattern and are not simply random sounds. They belong to the javelina's overall behavior model. Other behaviors, such as mutual grooming or foraging for food, are equally distinctive, contributing to a complete profile. In some instances a physical characteristic is responsible for behavioral traits. The javelina's dorsal scent gland, for example, is involved in several aspects of the animal's daily life.

Javelina herd behavior seems to follow a group-living pattern more like that of primates than of other North American hoofed mammals. Sowls, who studied javelinas for many years, realized certain noises, often quiet enough to be inaudible to listeners in the wild, might be heard among captive animals. He accordingly set up pens in which to record these "conversations."

The sounds can be separated into two groups. The first set relates to cohesiveness, either between mother and offspring or in bringing the herd together. The other group is defensive, comprising warnings or calls for aggression toward assumed enemies. Javelinas will grunt repetitively in a low-pitched tone to stay in touch with each other. This noise can become a frantic barking or "woofing" if they are distressed or trying to reassemble the herd when danger is lurking. The most dramatic warning is an aggressive popping of the teeth, an alarming noise, like the sound of two bones hit together very rapidly, that can be heard half a mile away. As the animals bark loudly and pop their teeth they may mill around, scaring any intruder in the vicinity.

Javelina piglets in distress will squeal like baby domestic pigs. Some continue to vocalize this way into adulthood when upset. Mothers and their young purr gently and intimately together in the same contented way cats do. The piglets will stop purring to complain when the mother moves away or wants them to stop suckling.

Javelinas, except when threatened, are not clamorous. They are unlike their kin, the white-lipped peccaries, which, Emmons has written, move around in large herds producing "a continuous racket of bellowing, screaming, and loud tooth-clack which can be heard for several hundred meters." Young white-lipped peccaries in the herds call with loud retching noises.

In Texas, Arizona, and New Mexico, the size of herds varies. The number is determined in part by the food available and also by the type of vegetation interwoven with the edible plants. Commonly, smaller herds live in dense brush, while less-dense vegetation draw larger groups. In Arizona, herds average nine to twelve animals where hunting is permitted and twice that number where it is prohibited, such as in the Saguaro National Monument.

The herds are mixed in gender and age, and animals will stay together rather than switch from one herd to another until such time as one or two animals break away and form the nucleus of a new herd. However, research in both Texas and Arizona indicates that the reduction in herd size to four or five animals does away with herd integrity. In the daily search for food, the herd commonly splits into subgroups, especially in the height of summer, and individuals often wander away from the main herd for up to twelve hours. Adult females probably play an important role in creating new herds, and although there is no apparent leadership, the dominant animals within a group are generally male.

As the size of the herd varies, so does the size of its territory. In brush country the range will be well under a mile in any direction, but it will be three times as large in more open areas like the Trans-Pecos in Texas and the Tortolito Mountains in Arizona. Studies carried out by Texas Parks and Wildlife in South Texas brush lands indicate home ranges of two hundred to three hundred acres in thick brush riparian habitats, and five hundred to six hundred acres in less hospitable areas. Bedding areas may be shared where a herd's territory overlaps that of another herd but are used by one herd at a time rather than simultaneously.

The boundaries of such territories are defined by natural features such as waterholes, individual bushes, or even a sharp ridge or by scent left in chosen places, such as low tree limbs, not only to identify the boundary but also to leave a trail for any herd member lagging behind. Where a javelina has marked, the amber liquid from the gland turns dark on meeting the air and leaves a stain.

The advantages of moving in herds are readily apparent. By walking systematically, albeit unwittingly, the animals avoid retracing a path over spots where the food has already been devoured. As a group they can spot predators more easily, and they gain strength in numbers to repel attacks if the need arises. As the perceived enemy approaches, the herd will scatter in every direction making further attempts of capture too challenging. Not least of the advantages, younger members of the herd can learn life skills from the examples provided by their elders. The two disadvantages of this lifestyle are the sound and smell of the herd, which attract attention, and the easy spread of diseases.

JAVELINAS

Daily routine varies according to season. On winter mornings a herd will bask in the sunshine until it reaches a comfort level that encourages the animals to get up and feed. The cooler the weather, the longer the feeding period, up to several hours at a stretch. In the summer they are crepuscular, feeding near dawn and dusk. In West Texas they have been spotted eating through the coolest hours of night during the summer months. They start their daily routine at daybreak and by midmorning head for resting places, walking the extra distance to the spots they know provide the most comfort. During the hottest hours of the day they stop feeding. Javelinas in the arid Tucson Mountains of southern Arizona feed early in the morning until the temperature climbs to about 32°C, then seek out the cooler canyons until the temperature drops again in the evening.

At night they seek out something more substantial: a rocky overhang, a cave, or shallow hollows in the heavy brush. In the colder months three or four of them may lie huddled close together for warmth, overlapping as they stretch out on their sides or bellies, feet out in front, unable to curl their inflexible spine. In summer, when cool air becomes necessary, they even push away their young. They select for safety as well as comfort, with a drainage source close by and a corner reserved for toilet purposes; captive javelinas reserve a defecation corner in their pen. The fecal droppings are not always left in a single spot in the wild. This distribution allows researchers to use them to determine herd boundaries and daily pathways by leaving colored glass beads in feeding areas to be swallowed by the animals and later deposited in toilet areas.

During the day small groups break from the herd to forage. If food is plentiful, javelinas scatter over a wide area, preferring to seek out food on flat land along wash bottoms, avoiding where possible hillsides, especially rocky ones, that narrow to a bare peak. They never eat voraciously, but instead hold down the staple prickly pear with their front feet, peeling off one side to reach the juicy pulp. They opt for plants with fewer spines, although the spines seem to do no harm. When vegetation is abundant after rain, observers in Arizona have noted the animals ignore standing pools of water, though in higher and less green environments they enjoy sipping from streams. Javelinas share waterholes with other creatures. Their behavior varies according to whether friend or foe stands close at hand. They ignore cottontails and jackrabbits, while they may attack foxes. If young are in the herd, they sound a warning at a bobcat's approach. They avoid snakes even more firmly. Researchers pass around a story in which a rattlesnake drove javelinas away from a waterhole by buzzing at them, but they returned cautiously minutes later to drink from the other side.

Although eating and drinking, along with resting, constitute a sizable portion of the daily routine, javelinas—like other animals—have other pursuits. Living in a herd generates social activities, and while some of the behaviors suggest sexual foreplay, they are often simply gestures of friendship. Javelinas enjoy licking and nibbling each other gently, or rubbing snouts together and affectionately dabbing the other's scent gland, nuzzling with the snout resting on the animal's head or neck. This nuzzling sometimes becomes more vigorous, with two javelinas simultaneously standing head to tail rubbing the sides of their heads on the area of each other's rumps and rear legs, either as pleasure in itself or as a means of grooming each other. They also scoop up sand against their bellies or wallow in the dust to clean themselves. Young animals, no less than young humans, pay less attention to grooming than do adults.

Male javelinas reach sexual maturity at forty-six to forty-seven weeks, females at thirty-three to thirty-four weeks, and at times the grooming prefaces a more romantic turn of events. A male and female javelina greet each other nose to nose, then sniff each other's scent gland before moving to more sexually relevant parts of the body and wooing each other with low sounds. They may copulate within fifty yards or so of the other members of the herd, who show no apparent interest in the action, and the whole sequence takes as little as ten minutes or so. Biologists have studied the sexual behavior of javelinas extensively, addressing such interests as the number of mountings unrelated to reproduction and whether males mate with several females in the group to sustain the species or whether a single male within the herd is responsible for the next generation.

If the example of captive animals holds in the wild, one male will dominate in each group. He will hold the position longer in smaller groups than in larger ones. Usually, the outcome of one-on-one fighting determines leadership, for the victor is easily recognized. Young males, even before their long canines are grown to full length, will attack each other, clacking their jaws together in a fast staccato. They will flatten their ears back on their heads and butt each other in the face or lock jaws and swing each other around till both fall to the ground exhausted.

The various functions of the dorsal gland have received a lot of attention. The odor it releases is believed to be a way of achieving personal identity as well as distinguishing the herd. However, removal of the gland does not invariably spell trouble. One legendary male javelina became dominant when several females in his group were simultaneously in heat and forming partnerships with other males. His dorsal gland had been removed, but he contrived to replace his predecessor by severely biting his testicles.

When conception occurs, usually two offspring are delivered 142 to 151 days later. John Bissonette's research on javelinas in the Big Bend showed, as other studies have done, that the animals have no seasonal birthing period, but most arrivals tend to come between the midsummer months and late fall. In South Texas, however, births normally peak during February and March.

Javelina young are up on their feet within a few hours after birth and are able to follow their mother around, staying close by her side, a practice they will continue until they reach one year of age. In fact, the young will follow any adult javelina, assuming it to be their mother.

As a javelina mother has only two functioning teats situated at the tail end of her body, her piglets will usually stand while nursing, or sometimes kneel. At birth the young weigh about a pound. This body weight increases to between four and six pounds with frequent nursing, and they start eating solid food at several weeks.

The young, which actively work to get attention, flop on the ground in front of the mother when she is searching for food, demanding a "rub down," a nuzzling of flank or belly. They learn to demand early, for mother javelinas are negligent from a human standpoint. They neither clean their babies nor offer much attention when nursing; they make no protest if another member of the herd snaps at their offspring; and while they will defend their babies from any likely attacker, even to the point of charging and making a loud objection, they have been seen to abandon their young if the herd is threatened. A piglet's protests, as it cries in desperation, may further attract the attention of any would-be predator. In the 1890s, a member of the International Boundary Survey team took time away from surveying for a hunting sortie. He reported wounding a female javelina standing with her young amid a herd: "Although she squealed loudly, the remainder of the band rushed off and left her. A moment later, we came upon her among the bushes and cactuses, but she arose and escaped from us without attempting to defend her young which were no larger than cottontail rabbits."

Javelinas raised in captivity engage in plenty of play and camaraderie. During the first few weeks they demand fre-

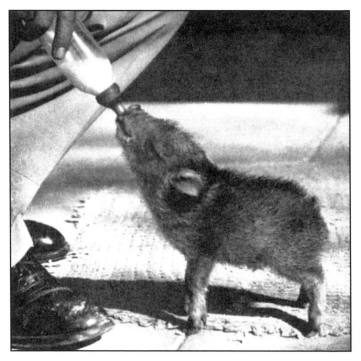

■ Javelina piglet only a few days old. Photograph by Bob Housh-
older, from Knipe, *The Javelina in Arizona.*

quent nursing periods, but if the mother is fed an adequate
diet, they can reach a threshold weight that gives them more
time for independence. Weaning seems to be managed
without conflict. Researchers have noted that the piglets
suckle whenever they want and for however long they want.
Until they are twelve to sixteen weeks old, they expend most
surplus energy running and leaping, chasing each other,
bumping head to head in mock fights, and spinning around
each other in circles or rolling over and over. Their play fos-
ters life skills in self-defense, cooperation, and ultimately
independence.

These skills, essential in the wild, hold them in good
stead when they venture into populated areas, such as sub-

urbs, where they sense no threat. In the same way they approach garbage cans in national parks, they will prowl residential districts hunting for food. In Arizona cities they are becoming a pest. Leaflets warn householders to secure all garbage and make sure edible garbage is beyond the animals' reach, to keep bird seed and pet food out of the way, and even to avoid using horse manure as fertilizer because it harbors tempting grubs and other insects. Shrubbery providing cover must be trimmed, and openings beneath buildings and mobile homes should be closed. Javelinas will root for spring bulbs (residents are advised to plant toxic iris or narcissus rather than tasty tulips) and eat fruit that drops from trees. Solar-powered electric fences, or less sophisticated wooden ones, will keep them out, and loud yelling or banging will scare them off. Because javelinas hate dogs, which remind them of the much-hated and feared coyote, dogs must be kept out of harm's way.

The trouble javelinas cause in urban settings is not vindictive, nor is the way they will muddy stock tanks when they wallow in them on the range in the hot summer months. Now, both through the investigations of scientific researchers and because of a more pragmatic approach to creatures of the wild, we better understand javelina behavior.

Hunting and Harvesting

THROUGHOUT THE Southwest mounted peccary heads are gathering dust at the back of garages or over fireplaces in dens. Although they document their owners' success in the hunt, they are not conventionally attractive. They offer an exaggerated and frightening appearance, as though declaring they put up a good fight before succumbing to the bullet or arrow that ended their life. Other trophies, especially deer, generate admiration or sympathy; but javelinas look singularly deserving of their fate.

As frontier days drew to a close and the United States took on an increasingly urban face, hunting became a sport rather than a means of keeping food on the table. Two late-nineteenth-century visionaries voiced their fear that hunting would lead to wide-scale slaughter of wildlife, threatening the country's natural heritage. Ernest Thompson Seton, a naturalist, artist, and author, drew attention to the crisis by writing animal tales to instill a love of nature in his young readers. He took the same message to adults, especially in his *Lives of Game Animals*. Today his writing seems cloying and almost condescending, but his warnings to respect and protect animals from extinction continue to resonate. "In the palmy days of the '50's and '60's, yes, even as late as the early '80's," he wrote, referring to the nineteenth century, "peccaries abounded in much of Texas; and were particularly plentiful in the southern part of the State, where low, dense thickets covered much of the country. Then came the Destroyer, the sordid white man with his destructive weapons.

■ Javelinas have poor eyesight but good senses of smell and hearing.
Wyman Meinzer

■ Javelinas communicate with a range of sounds from clicks and grunts
to loud barks. *Larry Ditto*

■ Javelinas spend most of their day eating and drinking. *Steve Bentsen*

■ Javelinas have no fear of water. *Mike Searles*

■ Javelinas enjoy licking and nibbling each other gently, or rubbing snouts together and affectionately dabbing the other's scent gland.
Steve Bentsen

■ Young javelinas stay near their mother until they are a year old.
Gary Kramer

■ Herds protect the young, but many are lost to predators.
Wyman Meinzer

■ Males compete noisily for dominance in the herd. *Gary Kramer*

■ Although omnivorous, javelinas prefer forbs, fruits, and beans often found beneath tall grass. *Mike Searles*

■ Natural enemies, a javelina and a coyote share a food drop. *Nancy Haggard*

■ Herds may number from a few animals to forty or fifty. *Larry Ditto*

■ When javelinas seem to be watching, more likely their keen hearing is coming into play. *Russell Graves*

■ In Arizona, javelina habitat is often rugged, mountainous country.
Sam and Mary Cissell

■ At a watering hole, javelinas shove and squeeze for the best spot.
Steve Bentsen

■ Javelinas can become accustomed to humans and allow them to approach closely. *Nancy Haggard*

■ Javelinas range over about a third of the state of Arizona, and their distribution is extending northward. *Nancy Haggard*

The territory of the little Pigs rapidly shrank." This comment surely refers to the market hunting of javelinas for their tough hide.

President Theodore Roosevelt took a more direct course of action. On his first trip to the frontier West in 1885, when he fulfilled an ambition to shoot a buffalo in the Dakotas, he was overwhelmed by the destruction he saw. Although we recognize now that habitat damage cannot be blamed on hunting, Roosevelt believed indiscriminate deforestation had come about at the hands of the "swinish game-butchers," the wildlife hunters who killed for sport. Buffalo were slaughtered principally for their hides and tongues, and as a means of taking away the American Indians' food source. When he returned to the East, he and a group of his friends founded the Boone and Crockett club, dedicated to preserving the American wilderness. Ever the realist, he made quite clear that he felt putting a halt to hunting altogether was sentimental. A middle path had to be found.

In April 1892 Roosevelt visited cousins of his wife in South Texas, hoping to bag a javelina along the Frio River. At the ranch house where he stayed, he learned that the last group in the area had been slaughtered the year before. When he heard of a small herd thirty miles to the south, he rode out to see for himself. He later recollected the scenery he enjoyed on his horseback ride to the Nueces River. He and his companion took along a well-fed ranch hound and a skin-and-bones javelina dog borrowed from a Mexican goatherder. All day they searched. "At last, after several false alarms, and gallops which led to nothing, when it lacked but an hour of sundown we struck a band of five of the little wild hogs. They were running off through the mesquites with a peculiar hopping or bounding motion, and we all, dogs and men, tore after them instantly." After charging at the group, the sow "stopped and stood still, chattering her teeth savagely, and I jumped off my horse and dropped her dead with

JAVELINAS

■ Mounted javelina head in the study of Theodore Roosevelt's home. *Courtesy Theodore Roosevelt Collection, Harvard College Library.*

a shot in the spine over the shoulders." The boar was their next target. "All the while his teeth going like castanets, with a rapid champing sound. I ran up close and killed him by a shot through the back-bone where it joined the neck. His tusks were fine." To this day a javelina trophy hangs on the wall of Roosevelt's home library at Sagamore Hill on Long Island, New York.

Roosevelt and Seton appealed for a simultaneously compassionate and pragmatic attitude, allowing hunting as acceptable, while wanton slaughter bode ill for the future. Neither discussed the commercial benefits that might accrue from dealing in javelina hides. This practice is outlawed now in the United States, but the economic value of hides and, to a lesser extent, bristles has been acknowledged since the 1880s. Texas fell into line with New Mexico and Arizona,

52

affording the javelina protection as a game animal in 1939 when the 46th Texas Legislature passed House Bill No. 884 with a vote of 127 to 5 in the House and by 25 votes to 4 in the Senate. The law effectively halted trading in skins taken from the javelinas killed in the state.

The Hide Trade

■ The situation in South America is somewhat different from that of North America. In several countries hides remain a source of income for hunters. The trade has taken a significant toll on the peccary population, with fluctuating markets driving the price up and down. Between 1969 and 1979 Peru exported 11,492,963 collared peccary skins and 821,899 white-lipped peccary skins. The three extant species of peccary all live in South America, and the highest quality skin, which comes from the javelina or collared peccary, commands the highest price even though it is the smallest. A sobering monograph prepared by the International Union for Conservation of Nature and Natural Resources in the early 1990s reveals that in 1988 West Germany alone imported 160,391 collared peccary skins, and the income was calculated as $30 million. Perhaps a million dollars reached the hands of the rural hunters, and a further $1.5 million were shared by South American intermediaries. The balance remained in the West German economy. During the 1980s some skins were probably smuggled out of Brazil, although the practice was banned. Peru continued as a major exporter until Argentina took the questionable honor. Bolivia and possibly Venezuela have also participated in the trade.

In 1990 when a ban on exporting hides was imposed in Argentina, the chief conduit for Bolivian and Paraguayan hides, the revenue fell in all three countries. Over the years, the former West Germany led the field of importers, making most of the skins into equestrian leather products. Japan, the

United States, and Italy were also customers, transforming the skins into a variety of leather goods. The highest prices were paid for javelinas, fetching as much as eight dollars each in Peru in 1990. At the same time, the white-lipped specimens raised five dollars apiece. The Chacoan hide, thin almost to the point of translucency, attracted little interest among overseas buyers, which, considering its endangered status, may be considered a blessing. Besides the hides used abroad, the number of domestic uses is impressive. Indigenous peoples in Latin America work the skins into a wide range of products, including drums, covers for arrow quivers, chairs, and occasionally boots.

In rural South America javelina meat is more valuable than hides in local markets, but the hides are significantly more important to the national economy. Despite legislation to prohibit sales, the laws are hard to enforce and low on the list of priorities. When prices are low, the demand lessens; but even when prices peak, hide sales have not been the primary cause of population decline. Other factors, especially land clearing for agriculture and human settlement, share the blame. The relationship between animals and people is always close, always different. In South America javelinas are a source of revenue and protein, and social anthropologists have recorded how the animals are woven into the cultural fiber of traditional life. In the American Southwest they are neophytes. No javelina silhouettes appear on American Indian pottery, and no images are woven into fabric or basketry; they aren't included in tales or songs. They made their way into the region just a few short generations before the European presence disrupted traditional tribal life. Animals nudge their way into folklore, playing a benevolent or malevolent role unrelated to their status in the wild. Thus the javelina becomes on the one hand an unusual pet, and on the other a monster as frightening as Grimm dogs guarding the tinderbox.

Hunting and Harvesting

In Dimmit County in South Texas the javelina played such an important role a century ago that legend and fact have become intertwined. The name of the weekly newspaper, the *Carrizo Springs Javelin,* immortalizes the thousands of martyred javelinas that saved the area from economic ruin. The paper began publication as a two-page home-printed effort and became widely read and respected during the tenure of a succession of editors, including a school principal who would race to his office during recess to put the next issue to bed. Another editor was persuaded to take office with the promise of free passes to attend shows and ride the railroad.

To this day Dimmit County is a sparsely populated area in South Texas. It was among the first places to profit from the development of barbed wire and became optimistic about expanding its economic base with livestock. Then in 1885 a devastating drought took hold of the region. By the following summer the ranchers who had depended on surface water for their herds found themselves ruined when the springs, creeks, and even the rivers dried up. Few wells were in place, and the seasonal grass did not grow. The cattle perished, and a drop in the price of wool left neighboring sheep raisers in dire straits. The one hundred and thirty thousand head of sheep in the county in 1880 decreased to five thousand within ten years.

A coincidence lessened the curse. Northern furriers became interested in javelina hides about the same time the drought became most destructive, and the Javelina War began. Ranchers and farmers in Dimmit County learned of a hide buyer in Laredo who was willing to pay twenty-five cents for each skin. Soon, thousands of javelina hides were hauled by wagon to the border town. Almost immediately the price rose, first to fifty cents and then to eighty cents. Traffic increased sharply, and the trade was formalized when a local merchant, J. L. McCaleb, printed an advertisement in

JAVELINAS

The Javelin, which he then owned and edited. The advertiser offered to pay between thirty cents and a dollar per javelina hide, according to size. McCaleb, whose main line of business was the local general store, also reached an agreement with a San Antonio wholesaler. The deal involved trading groceries for hides. Although citizens elsewhere in the drought-ridden region sought state assistance, the folk in Dimmit county took to the countryside with their guns. With little effort they could raise two or three dollars a day, more than enough to keep body and soul together. Enterprising hunters could earn as much as fifteen dollars a day. Customers bought all they needed at McCaleb's Mercantile Company, paying with large hides and receiving small ones in return when change was due.

After the drought ended in 1887, the cattle business started anew. Peter Tumlinson Bell, who lived through the period and whose lifelong memories were published by his grandson, recalled a lifelike mounted javelina fixed to the front wall of the newspaper office. The entrepreneurial McCaleb was undaunted when his fortunes changed. As the market for javelina hides dwindled, he invited his readers and customers to help fulfill a new demand—buckhorns to serve as knife handles.

San Antonio, Texas, was one of the hubs of the hide trade. More than a dozen dealers were listed in the 1880s in Morrison & Fourmy's *General Directory for the City of San Antonio,* trading in small shops in and around Military Plaza. H. P. Attwater wrote that Messrs. Cohen & Co. claimed to handle more than thirty thousand javelina hides around 1888, paying up to eighty cents for a good example. The hides were transported to the East Coast and shipped from there across the Atlantic Ocean to Europe, where they were transformed into gloves and brushes. The boom was short-lived. Within a few years warehouses were piled high with seasonal leftovers worth less than thirty cents apiece.

Another outcome was a decline in javelina numbers in Texas, especially to the west in the Trans-Pecos. This decline in turn raised the hide value again, so by 1917 the prices peaked at a dollar and fifty cents for a large skin, giving "Sunday hunters" a profitable as well as pleasurable day out. In Castolon, a small town in the Big Bend, La Harmonia store catered to area ranchers and miners as well as being a gathering place for Mexican hunters and traders. Clifford Casey's account of the store describes how during the winter months grocery and medical merchandise had to be squeezed close as furs were piled as high as they had been in frontier trading posts. Javelina hides fetched seventy-five cents from wholesalers, the same price as wildcats and opossums and close to three times the price of Mexican goatskins.

The next surge in demand came during the Depression, when hunters were paid a dollar for a javelina hide, enough to put food on the family table. Americans began to cross the border to buy hides from Mexicans, who kept bands of "scarred and rangy dogs" to corner the animals and make them easier to shoot. Professional operators soon edged out the smaller dealers.

Tom Neal of Uvalde probably handled the most hides in South Texas during the 1930s. In 1936 and 1937 he bought and sold fifteen thousand javelina hides a year, mostly from Mexico. He also bought from Alfredo Santos, a dealer in Laredo, who in turn dealt with hide traders in Monterrey, Mexico. Neal's hides were sold to a New York glove manufacturer and brokered by a commissioned agent in the border town of Eagle Pass. The Tanners Hide Company in San Antonio imported thirteen hundred javelina hides from Mexico in 1939. Many were exported to France to become women's gloves. Strips of hide also became purses, bags, shoe tops, and other fine leather items. Various types of brushes were made from the bristles.

In Arizona the R. W. Bailey Company imported javelinas

from Mexico's western states and reckoned on clearing fifty thousand of them in 1933. They were shipped by trucks up to Tucson, then freighted to Galveston and transported by boat to New York to be distributed to manufacturers, who eagerly bought them for gloves and jackets.

Even as conservationists and legislators strove to terminate the sale of hides, hunters honed their skills on javelinas, which were widely viewed as vermin and exempt from the laws protecting deer, elk, and antelope as game animals. One of the earliest advocates for javelina protection, Charles Vorheis of the University of Arizona, wrote to the state game warden and his representative in 1919 about the desirability of protecting them: "The avidity with which men kill them is sufficient evidence that they are generally regarded as game." Knipe cites a former supervisor of the Colorado National Forest, which lay beyond the animals' range, who commented back in 1930, "That such a unique and harmless animal should be exterminated instead of being protected as a valuable species of our wildlife appears unthinkable." These men did not intend an absolute hands-off policy; rather, they favored regulating populations, so hunting javelinas remained a viable sport.

Hunting

■ When the hunting laws were redrafted, javelinas gained protection as game animals in Arizona in 1927, New Mexico in 1937, and Texas in 1939. In the late 1930s, the U.S. Fish and Wildlife Service estimated the total population in the three states at 49,820, with 35,100 in Texas, 14,320 in Arizona, and just 400 in New Mexico. Within six years the figures had increased.

Texas lagged twelve years behind Arizona in implementing game laws to protect javelinas because ranchers and farmers insisted javelinas maimed and killed dogs, fouled waterholes and left them unfit for cattle, and harmed range animals, including angora goats—which some still believe to be true. Those opposed to a closed hunting season or bag limit had loud and influential voices. Along the borderlands they claimed Mexicans widely hunted javelinas, and if the season were left open, those hunters were less likely to take deer. Similarly, javelinas were an important dietary item for ranch laborers. If limitations were imposed, the deer population would be decimated. The antiprotectionists lost the argument, and each of the three states now has a clear set of hunting regulations.

As one of the last frontier regions, Texas has a long tradition of organized sport hunting, even though javelinas did not fit into the official picture in the early days. In 1909 the first hunting license law was enacted, and five thousand licenses were sold. In 1917 the Game, Fish, and Oyster (GFO) Commission, precursor to the Texas Parks and Wildlife Department, added a game division. Six years later the Texas State legislature turned over all game revenue to the GFO Commission, and forty-five wardens were on staff to enforce conservation laws. By 1925 the number had been raised to a hundred wardens, and a long list of protective measures appeared in the penal code forming the basis of the subsequent conservation program. In their 1929 report the commission outlined successive measures taken over the previous half century to conserve Texas wildlife. They noted that although peccaries were still common in the south and southwestern portions of the state, their numbers were dwindling.

The commission's 1945 update on the distribution and management of the principal game birds and mammals of Texas lamented the peccary's diminished range. At that time the javelina was limited to the region south of San Antonio and westward along the Rio Grande into the Big Bend area and the vast spaces of Brewster and Presidio counties. Yet even as the report appeared, the commission was hearing from ranchers and farmers in several counties further to the northeast, mostly along or close to the old Highway 90, who had sighted javelinas on their land after several years' absence. The effects of legislation to protect the javelina were already becoming evident.

Javelina hunting was not widely popular during this period. The animals were hard to track down as they favored inaccessible terrain, and, even when hunters were victorious, many found the meat unpalatable. Two other facts further curbed hunting: First, 97 percent of Texas land is privately owned, and for years most of the javelina habitat lay on ranches where little or no hunting was allowed. Second, an absolute ban was placed on trading in hides. These restrictions, together with an annual bag limit of two animals, turned around the population decline.

Although it sounds like a paradox, javelina populations are increasing because of, not in spite of, hunting. Resource managers monitor the relationship between wildlife and vegetation with new technologies that allow them to fine tune programs developed before the computer age. Game laws are enforced as closely as the remote wide-open spaces permit, with those working in the field taking action when necessary. As a result, the loss of animal habitat to agriculture, building, and highway construction can be offset partially by experienced management.

Texas javelinas share their range with the western mule deer and southern whitetail, the preferred targets of hunters. Forty-three counties in Texas permit javelina hunting from October 1 to February 26, and the season is open year-round in almost fifty others. The state offers permits for hunting on public land and a license allowing hunters to bag game as legally stipulated. The cost of the license to hunt all game species is considerably lower for Texas residents than nonresidents. In the 2004 fiscal year, the Texas Parks and Wildlife Department sold almost sixty-eight thousand non-

■ Killed deer and javelina tied to Herbert Davenport's Ford. *Courtesy Texas State Library and Archives Commission.*

resident hunting licenses (year-round general licenses, year-round small game and exotic licenses, and five-day licenses to hunt small game and exotics). Hunting receipts add up to a sizable portion of the department's revenue but fluctuate from year to year. In 2004, for example, license and stamp endorsement sales amounted to almost 50 percent of the $128.2 million total budget.

In Texas landowners regulate access to the land, but the wildlife on it belongs to the people of the state. The annual drawing for the Public Hunt Program offered close to six thousand drawn hunt positions for the 2004–2005 season. Of these, 298 were for javelinas. Enthusiasts who have not been lucky in the drawing will sometimes ride out to the hunt area hoping a cancellation will give them a chance as standby hunters.

The Arizona javelina population has fluctuated. The 1920s and early 1930s saw two significant declines disrupt the legalized hunting schedule. The animals gained protection in 1929 when a single peccary could be bagged between November 1 and January 31. During the 1930s hunting was banned for several years, and a ban was threatened again during the 1940s. As settlement in the state increased, so did an interest in hunting. A survey by the National Forest Service found the javelina population had risen tenfold by 1950. The increase continued, and by the late 1990s the population had reached sixty thousand and ranged over a third of the state.

The general hunting license for residents of the state is $25.50, and for nonresidents more than four times that at $113.50. The javelina tag costs $17.50 for residents, and $75.00 for nonresidents. The Arizona Game and Fish Department issued 28,005 licenses for javelinas for the 2005 season, of which 11,757 were for general firearms, 6,537 for HAM (handgun, archery, or muzzleloaders), and 9,771 for archery only. Each hunter was restricted to one javelina per calendar year. The total javelina harvest for all three classes was 4,610 javelinas. The seasonal percentage of permits issued for each class is determined by the number of applicants in the preceding year and the hunters' success ratio. The Spring Hunt Guidelines describe management criteria. The number of permits issued is determined by the actual herd size, whether it is within the average range of eight to twelve animals, or above or below this figure. January is reserved for bow hunting, and the type of weapon and geographic location is taken into consideration during February.

Hunting and Harvesting

Javelinas in New Mexico number between three thousand and four thousand, almost identical to the number of black bears in the state. It dipped as low as about three hundred in the 1930s. Hunting did not proceed immediately after protective legislation was enacted in 1937, and the first sport hunt was conducted in 1963 when a hundred permits were issued for a nine-day season. Limited hunting continued with an increase in annual permits until 1968, when a severe snowfall decimated the javelina population and halted hunting until 1972. As in Texas, the license cost in the state is lower for residents than for nonresidents. Few permits are issued here. Besides the scheduled hunts in early February, a few are also issued for depredation or "population reduction hunts," scheduled when deer, antelope, elk, or javelinas have trespassed into the agricultural crops or damaged fences and other property.

Hunting Techniques

■ Dates and duration of hunting have changed over time, respecting the main breeding season and allowing hunters a sporting chance to find their quarry. Like deer, javelinas can successfully camouflage their presence, and tracking them is restricted to daylight hours. A flashlight would be a useless tool for locating them. The winter months are best for hunting, as javelinas rise early in the cooler weather to go about their business and begin foraging. By April the temperatures have risen and the animals have started to shed their bristles, making them less attractive to those planning to mount their trophy.

In hilly terrain experienced hunters like to begin the day by climbing to a high elevation and panning the landscape with binoculars. As the javelinas' senses of smell and hearing are a lot stronger than their vision, hunters know to approach the herd or subgroup from downwind, moving warily, step by step.

Many hunters enjoy the challenge of stalking the short-sighted animals before taking aim with bows, pistols, or muzzleloaders. Brandon Ray, writing for *Texas Parks and Wildlife Magazine,* captures the mood of a 1998 experience in the mountains of West Texas: "I could hear the noisy javelinas munching cactus all around me. From a distance my hunting partner and I had counted at least four 'javvies' through binoculars. . . . I crouched down to crawl through the thorny brush to try to get a close shot at one of the noisy porkers. The skunklike scent of several javelinas wafting through the brush indicated I was close. When I came to a small opening in the brush, I heard the sound of my partner's bow sending an arrow crashing into the rocks perhaps 50 yards up the creek." Ray keeps the skull of a large boar on the corner of his desk as a reminder.

Several hunting weapons are legally acceptable, although methods used in the past would be prohibited today. Felix Azare wrote lengthy descriptions of tracking javelinas in South America in the eighteenth century. Groups of local hunters followed the javelinas' paths, then built a hedge of branches on either side with a deep pit at the end and drove the animals toward their fate by yelling at them. In Texas even now, dogs add to the excitement of javelina hunting and are considered a valuable help, but they are banned by the conservation departments in New Mexico and Arizona and by two Apache tribes who have open season for javelinas on their reservations.

Back in the 1930s, Roosevelt asserted enthusiastically that the true way to kill peccaries was on horseback with a spear; O'Connor, also a dedicated hunter, agreed that "spearing the truculent little beast on foot would also be exciting, and might become a highly developed pastime." Spears are not among the legal weapons today.

Muzzleloading rifles and handguns, crossbows, and bow and arrow hunting all have their designated seasons. Due to

Hunting and Harvesting

the nature of javelinas and their poor eyesight, all of the "means of take" are considered. The annual limit on the bag by any weapon is one peccary in New Mexico and Arizona and two peccaries in Texas. During the 1990s the annual Texas javelina harvest averaged 18,700 animals, although these figures may be considered conservative.

The Internet has pervaded hunting no less than it has pervaded other commercial ventures. It is a boon to companies running private hunts, to guides who promote their service state by state, to hunting outfitters, and to those who market all the paraphernalia connected with the sport. One landowner in Texas offers two hogs and a javelina on all "hog hunts," pricing the trips from $195 for a care-for-yourself cabin to several hundred dollars for the luxury of having someone to cook, clean, guide, and clean the game. Another includes a bag of two javelinas, a bobcat, a mountain lion, and "all large varmints." That scathing term "varmint," defined in the Oxford English Dictionary as a "mischievous or discreditable person or animal," includes coyotes, rabbits, and rattlesnakes. As javelinas may be hunted year-round in many counties or when other game is off-limits, ranchers enjoy making a few extra dollars from groups who will spend $150 apiece for a three-day weekend, throwing in an old bunkhouse for the hours after sundown.

Each offer on the Internet sounds more tempting than the last. A site of five thousand acres secured behind a game fence, with spacious blinds, automatic feeders, and experienced guides awaiting the hunter's arrival, is becoming a standard rather than an exception. Clothing and sporting outfitters will arrange a hunting trip for aoudad sheep in a packet that flies customers to El Paso, drives them to a small West Texas town, and throws in a free javelina as a gesture of goodwill.

As the working week grows shorter, leisure hours grow longer and appetites crave new adventures. Sport hunting has spread far beyond the well-heeled elite who traveled to Africa and Asia or to barely accessible aeries in the northern Rockies. It has become a flourishing business in the American Southwest.

A century ago American Indian reservations were not on anyone's list of vacation spots, and traditional beliefs meant javelinas were not widely hunted or eaten there. Now, Apache tribes in Arizona welcome hunters to their reservation. Outsiders may buy permits to hunt with firearms or bow and arrow on the San Carlos Apache Reservation or the White Mountain Apache Reservation. White Mountain is world-renowned for elk hunting. A seven-day hunt, including a permit to bag an elk, costs $16,000 (whether or not one is successful) and a further $3,000 if the trophy animal exceeds a stipulated minimum size. There a first-rate animal fetches up to $15,000.

In the past, the Chiricahua Apaches believed dreams about peccaries were a bad omen, and their Central and Eastern bands refused the meat because javelinas ate snakes. The meat was taboo to the Western Apaches and Colorado River Yumas, but not to the Gila River Yumas. In the 1940s the White Mountain Apaches rejected javelinas as food despite the abundance of the animals on the reservation. However, the proscription was not held universally. Anthropologists studying the people of the Southwest early this century saw that the Papagos and, perhaps, the nearby Pima people killed and ate peccaries. A member of one Southern Chiricahua group described how their hunters surrounded brushy areas where javelinas were to be found, then rounded them up and killed them with a barrage of arrows. He added that they also ate the unborn peccaries.

The taste of the meat is debatable, though the younger the animal the more tender the meat. In a letter to an early issue of *Texas Parks and Wildlife,* a young Texan wrote: "The javelina meat is a special supper on our table. When it comes to cooking javelina, my own mother and grandmother are the best."

The consensus among those who enjoy javelina meat is that sows and yearlings are preferable and males older than two or three years make very tough eating. For others, tenderness does not make up for the taste. Reliving the experience, Jack O'Connor confessed that although the meat "looks beautiful—smooth, pink and appetizing . . . once you try to cook it, that rank odor begins to steal out of the pot. You gag. Presently you throw it away." O'Connor did not understand that the scent gland is attached to the hide and comes off when the animal is skinned.

Prior to 1600 Spaniards in the New World sent home many accounts of peccaries being kept, fattened and traded, and eaten at feasts. The meat was never universally acclaimed, though an 1894 issue of *Scribner's Magazine* suggested, perhaps a little daringly, "Lucky indeed will be the guest who shall be invited to partake of . . . stewed *jabelin*."

Father Nentvig, a German-born missionary spreading the gospel in Mexico in the eighteenth century, wrote, "In order to use its meat, hunters must carry a reed or hollow cane to insert in the navel the moment the pig falls dead, for this causes the vaporizing of the musk contained in this area. Otherwise, the musk taints all the flesh and no one can eat it regardless of how hungry one may be." This technique is no longer recommended. Instead, the animal needs to be skinned from the inside out, and the gland yanked off with the rest of the hair and its lining.

The writer Robert Mauermann reminisced: "We had tenderloin steaks from the saddle and baked the hams by digging a hole and building a fire in it until the ground was thoroughly hot; then we raked out the coals and ashes, lined the hole with grape leaves from a vine overhanging the waterhole, putting the two hams in and covering them with more grape leaves. The hole was then filled with hot ashes and a good fire kept on top all night. In the morning they were thoroughly cooked and delicious." A woman who grew up on the King Ranch fondly remembers javelina tamales as a Christmas Eve tradition.

In *Unmentionable Cuisine,* Calvin Schwabe, who spent thirty years gathering recipes from around the world, presents exotic dishes of "animal origin," which may soon reach American palates. Dogs, cats, rodents, reptiles, insects, and other land invertebrates are even less appealing than peccaries. Schwabe advances recipes beyond the hunter's rough and ready barbecue. He notes that javelina meat is quite dry; but if thin sheets of fat are tied on the surface before cooking, a practice called larding, the meat can be prepared using any recipe for suckling pig. For example, a Chinese recipe involves stuffing the javelina with fruit such as fresh Chinese dates, wrapping it in straw matting, then encasing it in clay (or perhaps simply aluminum foil), and baking it at 325 degrees for about five hours, followed by optional steaming. A Spanish favorite calls for rubbing the body cavity liberally with garlic, then filling it with a handful or two of chopped parsley, assorted herbs, and some chopped onion. Once prepared, the javelina is placed in a roasting pan, covered with an equal quantity of wine and water, topped with a piece of lard, and baked for an hour before being basted repeatedly with olive oil and meat drippings till it is crisp and golden brown. Schwabe also supplies a number of Russian, German, and western Mediterranean recipes, which are hard to read, let alone to eat.

Jerry Cooke, who works with the Texas Parks and Wildlife Department, recommends cooking in a pit barbecue, or grinding the meat to make sausage, which acquires a distinctly European flavor. For those not disposed to hunt, javelina dishes can sometimes be chosen off the menus of restaurants in small towns along the border.

This emphasis on javelina meat and hides may suggest

more interest in the dead animals than in the live ones. Generations of students at the Crystal City High School in South Texas would refute this. Their athletic teams were always known as the "Javelins." Always, that is, until ethnic pride translated the name to befit the largely Hispanic population, and the "Javelinas" became a symbol of pride.

Human Relations

IF THE JAVELINAS are a symbol of pride at the Crystal City High School, they are no less so at the nearby town of Kingsville. The Texas A&M campus here is the only college in the country to have selected the javelina as a mascot. The school was organized in 1917 when the legislature appropriated funds for the South Texas Normal School. World War I intervened before the doors were opened, and the first classes were held in the 1920s. By that time the school had become the South Texas State Teachers College. As the mission of the college changed and expanded, it became first the Texas College of Arts and Industries and later the Texas A&I University. In 1993 the school joined the Texas A&M University system.

The javelina appears in various art forms created by former students, none more striking than the sculpture standing at the campus entrance. Alumni raised more than $70,000 for the "Leaders of the Pack," a sculpture of the animals surrounded by South Texas flora. It was created by Armando Hinojosa, who became a teacher for gifted and talented art students in Laredo. The sculpture was unveiled in 1986 as a Texas Sesquicentennial event.

The "hoggy" logo adopted for the university banner in 1965 was designed by Amado Maurilio Pena Jr., a former high school teacher who has become one of the best-known artists in the Southwest. Elsewhere on campus is a life-sized javelina built out of plowshare parts by Tom Shelton in 1968. Each metal strip represents an accurate anatomical fea-

■ Javelina sculpture on the grounds of Texas A&M University–
Kingsville. *Courtesy Texas A&M University–Kingsville.*

ture. The glittering model was presented as a gift to Bee
County and later brought to the university to stand in Athletic Hall, a large building surrounded by an iron fence with
javelina-head cartouches set between the rails.

As well as these artistic tributes, the theme has been
familiar in other guises since early days. An Old Javelina Cafe,
for example, became the A&I Biology Department; and a
Javelina Confectionery and Snack Bar was opened in 1929.

The javelina became an icon because of its fighting spirit
and because of its reputation for coming to render aid when

a member of the herd is attacked. It has certainly brought a goodly share of luck, for no NCAA Division II school has had so many All-American honorees. At least one has been named every football season for the past thirty years.

The choice of a javelina as mascot was made back in 1925 when "Aggie" Manning, a business professor for whom the Administration Building was named on the school's fiftieth birthday, brought three baby javelinas to a pen on the north side of the Forum auditorium. He was charged with "civilizing" the small animals, which were constantly found wandering around campus on the site of a former onion patch.

The three were known as Joe, Bob, and Baby. Bob was the friendliest, and Baby the only female. When events at the Forum were less than compelling, the audience could watch the trio playing in their sty. On hot days classes were held often in the covered open patio near the javelinas, and whether by accident or intent, the animals made a habit of nosing their way out and disrupting the students and their instructor. Bob occasionally came close and threw the coeds into a real or feigned panic.

The student newspaper, *The South Texan*, faithfully printed every story about the javelinas that came its way. On one occasion, prior to a game between the college and the 14th Field Artillery, Baby wandered under a car as the driver paid his entrance fee. The little animal was seriously injured, and caretaker Professor Warren was called to administer first aid. After several anxious days, during which students were updated with frequent bulletins, she made a full recovery.

Worse was yet to come. Dr. Robert Barstow Cousins, first president of the college, was walking out in the pasture on a Sunday evening when he was attacked by one of the mascots. The *Kingsville Record News*, protecting the anonymity of the perpetrator in their September 28, 1929, edition, reported that Dr. Cousins received three gashes in the calf of his left leg in the javelina's first rush and a bite on his left hand when he tried to dislodge the "maddened hog." Usually the animal was playful, but this time it bit fiercely, and the president had to make a tourniquet with his belt before hobbling home. The family physician was called to dress the wounds. Suspecting the worst, the animal was killed and the head rushed to Austin in a record-breaking drive by W. G. Campbell, the registrar of the college. The javelina was found to be rabid, and the president had to undergo a long and painful series of Pasteur shots. The faculty voted to be rid of the mascots, but Dr. Cousins saved their bacon, as it were, by protesting, "I was on that javelina's territory, and he put up a grand fight. The animal is typical of this section of Texas and it certainly has the fighting spirit that would be exemplified in our athletic teams."

After the first three mascots ended their days in service to the college, a series of single animals succeeded them. Among the best remembered was Scrappy, captured in 1958, who destroyed a handler's boots and tried to stop him from loading the cannon for the football game. Porky was the campus icon from 1968 to 1990, a far longer period than the customary ten-year life span javelinas enjoy in the wild.

These chapters have chronicled the lifestyle of javelinas and their kin and people's attitudes toward them. Down in Kingsville, they are a welcome part of college life. To hunters they provide an opportunity to enjoy the great outdoors without too much cost or pressure. In state and national parks we hope to catch a glimpse of javelinas. We are tickled to see them shuffle and scuffle around seeking a mouthful of dusty vegetation, apparently oblivious to our presence, and certainly unafraid.

Javelinas, like every other living creature, have their place. Traditionally, it is out in the wild, but in Tucson and a growing number of cities they are becoming a nuisance. Their wanderings do not take them from one bush or clump of cactus to another, to a stream bank or the cool shade of a cliff overhang. Instead, they prowl through suburban neighborhoods and follow their snouts to restaurants, looking for tidbits from garbage cans or pet bowls. As they explore their surroundings, they are apt to damage the landscape, eat the plants, and break sprinkler systems in carefully planned yards. The Arizona Game and Fish Department has prepared a pamphlet to advise people on how to cope with them.

The javelina's adaptation to suburban life is a strange turn of events. Conservationists complain that human settlement and the accompanying trappings like highways and houses are displacing wildlife. Now, though, there seems to be a hint of retaliation. Javelinas, the mildest of creatures, are showing an unexpected determination to make the best of life wherever their path may take them.

A few years into the twentieth century, in an article about the mammals of New Mexico, Vernon Bailey pleaded for javelina protection: "Although not important game animals, peccaries make fairly good food, and the skins and heads of old males are interesting trophies. Far more important, however, is the value of interesting native animals, unique in structure and habits, with a precarious foothold in one little corner of our great country that will soon disappear forever if not given careful protection." As the list of endangered and protected animals grows, javelinas will probably survive while hunting persists as a sport.

The revised edition of *Javelinas and Other Peccaries,* by the late Lyle K. Sowls, a former professor of the University of Arizona, is a splendid all-round source of information on the three species of peccaries and as such has been an invaluable resource. The book was my primary guide as I wended my vicarious way through scrubland and mountains to understand the javelina's way of life. In addition to this "bible," I read other helpful and enjoyable accounts by naturalists, park rangers, conservationists, missionaries, travelers, militia, researchers, journalists, geologists, and historians.

Every story has to have a beginning, and Walter W. Dalquest and Gerald E. Schultz's *Ice Age Mammals of Northwestern Texas,* along with *Pleistocene Mammals of North America* by Bjorn Kurten and Elaine Anderson, provided a geological base showing how long the peccaries and their ancestors have roamed around the western hemisphere.

In describing the animals they observed on a daily basis, John Bissonette, G. I. Day, T. Knipe, and more recently Eric Hellgren, Jane Packard, Kimberley Babbitt, R. L. Lochmiller, and their colleagues, along with several others, have contributed detailed regional studies on the range, habitat, diet, and behavior of javelinas in particular areas.

After German missionaries' reports whetted their appetites (literally, in some cases), records from the nineteenth century were more varied, and quite often I was entertained by their improbability. Some of the authors, given to exaggeration and imagination, deserve anonymity. All the same, it would be a pity to miss naming J. O. Pattie, who traveled west from Kentucky and almost glamorized javelinas in the "personal narrative" of his great adventure in the 1830s. Other travelers, from Mary Austin Holley and Frederick Olmsted to the Texas boosters who whistled through the state on the alert for anything novel, immortalized peccaries in their different ways. It was helpful to track on a map the javelina sightings described by Lieutenant Emory for the 34th Congress of the United States and by E. A. Mearns's bulletin for the National Museum on the "Mammals of the Mexican Boundary of the United States." Both took an earnest and factual approach.

My favorite accounts were on the human, rather than the scientific aspects. Robert Mauermann wrote *The Javelina in Texas* for the Texas Game and Fish Commission in 1943. The bland title belies the wealth of fascinating information and conjecture he included. Likewise, Clifford Casey's *Soldiers, Ranchers, and Miners in the Big Bend* described the 1920s frontier store, piled high with animal skins and everything a person could possibly want when living along the border, far from any town—all of which gave insight into the economy of javelinas. This information was supplemented by articles and books about Dimmit County in South Texas and the reminiscences of Peter Tumlinson Bell.

The economic aspect of javelinas was the focus of two enlightening studies. W. L. R. Oliver edited the eye-opening *Pigs, Peccaries, and Hippos: Status Survey and Conservation Action Plan* for the International Union for Conservation of

Nature and Natural Resources. Supplying even more detail, "The Peccary—With Observations on the Introduction of Pigs to the New World" by R. A. Donkin goes far beyond the scope of this book in describing the peccary's place among Indian groups in South America. Delwin E. Benson's edited *Wildlife Stewardship and Recreation on Private Lands* taught me about current approaches to wildlife resource management.

With so many books, so many articles, I have difficulty highlighting one at the expense of another. I have not space to identify all the useful sources I found, but two cannot be omitted. Ernest Thompson Seton, one of the most eclectic naturalists of the century, gathered earlier writings, then made his own assessment in *Lives of Game Animals.* No one, however, quite matched the "Wilderness Hunter," Theodore Roosevelt's description of a javelina hunt in South Texas included in his *Hunting Tales of the West.* Would that others today wrote with such confidence in their opinions and could reconcile conservation and sportsmanship so well. He was never too worried about the criticism of others and set pen to paper as easily as he spoke, always with a sense of minding the future at least as much as the past. Despite the many trophies adorning the walls at Sagamore Hill, among them a javelina head, he was an unambiguous advocate for America's wildlife.

■ SELECTED SOURCES

Allen, Joel A. *On Mammals Collected in Bexar County and Vicinity, Texas, by Mr. H. P. Attwater, with Field Notes by the Collector.* Bulletin of the American Museum of Natural History. Vol. 8. New York, 1896.

Audubon, J. J., and J. Bachman. *Quadrupeds in North America,* Vol. 1. New York: V. G. Audubon, 1852.

Azare, Felix. *Voyage dans l'Amerique Meridionale (1809),* cited in Part 2 of *Maximilian, Prince of Wied's Travels in the Interior of North America 1832–1834* reprinted in *Early Western Travels, 1748–1846,* ed. Reuben Gold Thwaites, Vol. 23. Cleveland: The Arthur H. Clark Co., 1906.

Babbitt, Kimberley J., and Jane M. Packard. "Parent-offspring conflict relative to phases of lactation." *Animal Behavior* 40 (1990): 765–73.

Bailey, Vernon. *Mammals of New Mexico.* North American Fauna No. 53. Washington, D.C.: USDA Bureau of Biological Survey, 1905.

Bell, Verner Lee, ed. *Memories of Peter Tumlinson Bell, 1869–1956.* Carrizo Springs, TX: Bell, 1980.

Benson, Delton E., Ross "Skip" Shelton, and Don W. Steinbach. *Wildlife Stewardship and Recreation on Private Lands.* College Station: Texas A&M University Press, 1999.

Bissonette, J. A. *Ecology and Social Behavior of the Collared Peccary in Big Bend National Park.* National Park Service Science Monograph. 16 (1982).

Bollaert, William. *William Bollaert's Texas,* Edited by W. Eugene Hollon and Ruth L. Butler. University of Oklahoma Press, 1956.

SELECTED SOURCES

Bracht, Viktor. *Texas in 1848*. Translated in 1849 by Charles Frank Schmidt. San Antonio: Naylor Printing Co., 1931.

Casey, Clifford B. *Soldiers, Ranchers, and Miners in the Big Bend*. Washington D.C.: U.S. Department of the Interior, National Park Service, 1969.

Cook, James H. *Fifty Years on the Old Frontier*. New Haven, CT: Yale University Press, 1933.

Dalquest, Walter W., and Gerald E. Schultz. *Ice Age Mammals of Northwestern Texas*. Wichita Falls, TX: Midwestern State University Press, 1992.

Day, G. I. *Javelina Research and Management in Arizona*. Phoenix: Arizona Game and Fish Department, 1985.

Donkin, R. A. "The Peccary—With Observations on the Introduction of Pigs to the New World." *Transactions of the American Philosophical Society* 75 no. 5 (1985).

Doughty, R. W. *Wildlife and Man in Texas: Environmental Change and Conservation*. College Station: Texas A&M University Press, 1983.

Ellisor, J. E., and F. Harwell. *Ecology and Management of Javelina in South Texas*. F. A. Report Series No. 16. Austin: Texas Parks and Wildlife Department, 1979.

Emmons, Louise H. *Neotropical Rainforest Mammals: A Field Guide*. 2nd ed. Chicago: University of Chicago Press, 1997.

Emory, Lieutenant W. H. *Report on the United States and Mexican Boundary Survey Made Under the Direction of the Secretary of the Interior*. Vol. 2 1857–1859. Washington, D.C.

Farm and Ranch (magazine). Dallas, TX, 1884.

Findley, James S. *New Mexican Mammals*. Albuquerque: University of New Mexico Press, 1987.

SELECTED SOURCES

Grant, Chapman. *Big Game of the Texas Border.* London: Zoological Society Bulletin, 1916.

Hellgren, Eric C., et al. "Peccary Demographics." *Journal of Wildlife Management* 59, no. 1 (1985).

Hernandez, Francisco. *Nova Plantarum, Animalium et Mineralium Mexicanorum.* Rome, 1651.

History of Texas. New York: Nafis and Cornish, 1844.

Holley, Mary Austin. *Texas.* Austin: Steck, 1935.

Ikin, Arthur. *Texas: Its History, Topography, Agriculture, Commerce, and General Statistics.* Waco: Texian Press, 1964. First published in 1841.

Ilse, Linda M., and Eric Hellgren. "Resource Partitioning in Sympatric Populations of Collared Peccaries and Feral Hogs in Southern Texas." *Journal of Mammalogy* 76, no. 3 (1995): 784–99.

Knipe, Theodore. *The Javelina in Arizona: A Research and Management Study.* Wildlife Bulletin no. 2. Phoenix: Arizona Game and Fish Department, 1956.

Kurten, Bjorn, and Elaine Anderson. *Pleistocene Mammals of North America.* New York: Columbia University Press, 1980.

Lochmiller, Robert L., et al. "Body Condition Indices for Malnourished Collared Peccaries." *Journal of Wildlife Management* 53, no. 1 (1989): 205–208.

Mauermann, Robert. "The Javelina in Texas." *Texas Game and Fish* 2 (1943): 1.

Mearns, E. A. "Mammals of the Mexican Boundary of the United States." *U.S. National Museum Bulletin* (Washington, D.C.: Smithsonian Institution) 56, no. 1 (1907).

SELECTED SOURCES

(Judge) Moses. Untitled article under pseudonym 'Sesom.' *San Antonio Express*, 1888.

Neal, B. J. "A Contribution on the Life History of the Collared Peccary in Arizona." *American Midland National* 61 (1959).

Nentvig, Juan. *Rudo Ensayo: A Description of Sonora and Arizona in 1764.* Translated by A. F. Pradeau and R. R. Rasmussen. Tucson: University of Arizona Press, 1980.

Nuttall, Thomas. "A Journal of Travels into the Arkansas Territory, During the Year 1819," reprinted in *Early Western Travels, 1748–1846*, ed. Reuben Gold Thwaites, Vol. 13. Cleveland: The Arthur H. Clark Co., 1905.

Oliver W. L. R., ed. *Pigs, Peccaries, and Hippos: Status Survey and Conservation Action Plan.* Gland, Switzerland: IUCN, 1993.

Olmsted, Frederick L. *A Journey Through Texas.* New York: Dix, Edwards, 1857.

Opler, M. *An Apache Life-Way: The Economic, Social, and Religious Institutions of the Chiricahua Indians.* Chicago: University of Chicago Press, 1941.

O'Connor, J. *Game in the Desert.* New York: Derrydale Press, 1939.

Packard, Jane, Kimberley J. Babbitt, Kathleen M. Franchek, and Paige M. Pierce. "Sexual competition in captive collared peccaries." *Applied Animal Behaviour Science* 29 (1991): 319–26.

Pattie, J. O. *The Personal Narrative of James O. Pattie of Kentucky.* Edited by T. Flint. Cincinnati: John H. Wood, 1833.

Pfefferkorn, Ignaz. *Sonora: A Description of the Province.* Translated by T. E. Treutlin. Albuquerque: University of New Mexico Press, 1949.

SELECTED SOURCES

Ray, Brandon. "Tiny Tuskers." *Texas Parks and Wildlife Magazine*, 1998.

Rea, A. M. "Resource Utilization and Food Taboos of Sonoran Desert Peoples." *Journal of Ethnobiology* 1 (1981): 69–83.

Reid, Mayne. *The Hunters' Feast or Conversations Around the Camp-fire*. London: C. H. Clark, 1860.

Roosevelt, Theodore. *Hunting Tales of the West*. Vol. 2. New York: Current Literature Publishing Co., 1907.

Schwabe, Calvin W. *Unmentionable Cuisine*. Charlottesville: University Press of Virginia, 1979.

Seton, Ernest T. *Lives of Game Animals*. New York: Doubleday, Doran, 1929.

Sowls, Lyle K. *Javelinas and Other Peccaries*. College Station: Texas A&M University Press, 1997.

Taylor, W. P., and W. P. Davis. "The Mammals of Texas." *Texas Game, Fish, and Oyster Commission Bulletin* (Austin) 27 (1947).

Texas Game, Fish and Oyster Commission. *Review of Texas Wildlife and Conservation: Protective Efforts from 1879, etc.* Austin, 1929.

Tidwell, Laura K. *Dimmit County Mesquite Roots*. Austin: Wind River Press, 1984.

Webber, Charles C. *Romance of Sporting: Wild Scenes and Wild Hunters*. Philadelphia: J. B. Lippincott & Co., 1876.

Weniger, Del. *Texas Explorers*. Vol. 2. Austin: Eakin Press, 1997.

Wetzel, Ralph M. "The Extinction of Peccaries and a New Case of Survival." *New York Academy of Sciences Annals* no. 288 (1977).